Collins

Extended Essay

Supervisor and Coordinator Handbook

Ashley Denham Busse and Michele Lackovic

for the IB Diploma Programme

William Collins' dream of knowledge for all began with the publication of his first book in 1819.
A self-educated mill worker, he not only enriched millions of lives, but also founded a flourishing publishing house.
Today, staying true to this spirit, Collins books are packed with inspiration, innovation and practical expertise.
They place you at the centre of a world of possibility and give you exactly what you need to explore it.

Published by Collins
An imprint of HarperCollins*Publishers*
The News Building, 1 London Bridge Street, London, SE1 9GF, UK

HarperCollins*Publishers*
Macken House, 39/40 Mayor Street Upper, Dublin 1, D01 C9W8, Ireland

Browse the complete Collins catalogue at
collins.co.uk

10 9 8 7 6 5 4 3 2 1

A catalogue record for this publication is available from the British Library.

ISBN 978-0-00-877031-0

Authors: Ashley Denham Busse and Michele Lackovic
Publisher: Catherine Martin
Product developer: Daniela Mora Chavarría
Development editor: Sonya Newland
Copyeditor: Mark Gadd
Proofreader: Catherine Dakin
Cover designer: Amparo Barreras (Kneath Associates)
Typesetter and illustrator: Six Red Marbles
Production controller: Alhady Ali
Printed and bound in the UK by Ashford Colour Ltd.

MIX
Paper | Supporting responsible forestry
FSC™ C007454

This book contains FSC™ certified paper and other controlled sources to ensure responsible forest management.

For more information visit: www.harpercollins.co.uk/green

Acknowledgements
With thanks to Abhinandan Bhattacharya at Finland International School, Race Course, Mumbai and Jill Meadow for their review comments.

The publishers gratefully acknowledge the permission granted to reproduce the copyright material in this book. Every effort has been made to trace copyright holders and to obtain their permission for the use of copyright material. The publishers will gladly receive any information enabling them to rectify any error or omission at the first opportunity.

We are grateful to the International Baccalaureate Organization for their permission to reproduce copyright material under licence, including the IB Learner Profile attributes, the Approaches to Learning skills, the Interdisciplinary frameworks, the Assessment Criteria, the IB Guidelines for the Extended Essay and the Guiding questions from the IB Extended Essay Guide © International Baccalaureate Organization, 2023.

Contents

The IB learner profile

The IB learner profile consists of ten key characteristics that the International Baccalaureate designed to help the students nurture and develop. These traits will help students become more well-rounded, empathetic, confident and self-aware, and equip students with valuable skills that extend well beyond the classroom.

The IB learner profiles

IB programmes aim to develop internationally minded people who, recognising their common humanity and shared guardianship of the planet, help to create a better and more peaceful world.

IB students strive to be:

Inquirers: We nurture our curiosity, developing skills for inquiry and research. We know how to learn independently and with others. We learn with enthusiasm and sustain our love of learning throughout life.

Knowledgeable: We develop and use conceptual understanding, exploring knowledge across a range of disciplines. We engage with issues and ideas that have local and global significance.

Thinkers: We use critical and creative thinking skills to analyse and take responsible action on complex problems. We exercise initiative in making reasoned, ethical decisions.

Communicators: We express ourselves confidently and creatively in more than one language and in many ways. We collaborate effectively, listening carefully to the perspectives of other individuals and groups.

Principled: We act with integrity and honesty, with a strong sense of fairness and justice, and with respect for the dignity and rights of people everywhere. We take responsibility for our actions and their consequences.

Open-minded: We critically appreciate our own cultures and personal histories, as well as the values and traditions of others. We seek and evaluate a range of points of view, and we are willing to grow from the experience.

Caring: We show empathy, compassion and respect. We have a commitment to service, and we act to make a positive difference in the lives of others and in the world around us.

Risk-takers: We approach uncertainty with forethought and determination; we work independently and cooperatively to explore new ideas and innovative strategies. We are resourceful and resilient in the face of challenges and change.

Balanced: We understand the importance of balancing different aspects of our lives – intellectual, physical, and emotional – to achieve well-being for ourselves and others. We recognise our interdependence with other people and with the world in which we live.

Reflective: We thoughtfully consider the world and our own ideas and experience. We work to understand our strengths and weaknesses to support our learning and personal development.

Approaches to Learning skills

The IB Approaches to Learning help students build skills to become a better student in all your IB classes. It focuses on five important skill areas – how you think, communicate, work with others, manage yourself, and conduct research. Instead of teaching these skills separately, your teachers work them into all your subjects. This creates a shared language across your classes and helps you become the kind of curious, knowledgeable and caring person the IB wants to develop. It also helps you understand your own learning style – not just what you are learning, but how you learn best. These are skills you will use long after school, in college and throughout your life.

Approaches to Learning skills

Thinking skills: question ideas, come up with creative solutions, use knowledge from one subject to help in another, and think about how learning happens

Social skills: work in teams, take the lead when needed, understand personal feelings and others', and resolve conflicts

Communication skills: get better and more confident at sharing ideas, listen to others, and understand people from different cultures

Self-management skills: keep track of work, use time wisely, stay focused, recover from setbacks, and find study methods that work

Research skills: know how to find reliable information, understand media messages, use information responsibly, and do honest academic work

Meet the authors

This resource is the combined work of two experienced and passionate IB educators who have held various roles within IB schools. They have both mentored countless students through successful research projects as extended essay supervisors, coordinators and literature teachers, and share a love of the IB and what it can bring to a school community. Please see a short introduction for each author below.

Ashley Denham Busse

Ashley Denham Busse is an IB Language A: literature teacher, IB Diploma Programme Coordinator, and former Extended Essay Coordinator at Suncoast Community High School in Palm Beach County, Florida. She has taught literature and writing for over 15 years at both the secondary and university levels.

A proud IB Diploma Programme graduate herself, Ashley is passionate about the IB's mission to create a more peaceful world. Using the IB frameworks, she encourages students to become active, compassionate members of our global society, fostering intercultural understanding and respect. She holds an M.A. in English from Florida State University and a PhD in English literature from the George Washington University.

Michele Lackovic

Michele Lackovic brings over 25 years of experience supervising and coordinating the extended essay. Michele combines classroom wisdom with expertise in digital research technologies. She leads professional development on ethical AI integration in education and is passionate about empowering students to navigate both traditional and emerging research methodologies.

Currently serving as the MYP Coordinator and an IB Literature and Theory of Knowledge teacher at Suncoast Community High School in Florida, she has mentored countless students through successful research projects. Michele's approach balances academic rigour with compassionate guidance — informed by watching her own two children recently complete the IB Diploma Programme. She holds degrees from Penn State and UCLA.

1 Overview and purpose of the extended essay

Welcome to the IB extended essay! This handbook will guide you through the process of mentoring students as they complete this unique and transformative part of the IB Diploma Programme. Extended essay coordinators and supervisors play a vital role in guiding students through their first substantial piece of independent academic research and writing. Your support will help them grow in confidence, maturity and skill; in turn, you will find that supervising an extended essay can be an immensely fulfilling endeavour for you as an educator.

This chapter covers the following:

- Overview, aims and learning outcomes of the extended essay
- The extended essay and the IB Diploma Programme

Overview, aims and learning outcomes of the extended essay

The IB extended essay is:

- an in-depth investigation of a topic of the student's choice, within one or two IB Diploma Programme subjects
- directed by the student under the supervision of a qualified member of school staff
- presented as a 4,000-word essay and a final reflection
- a research-informed piece of scholarly writing
- the result of about 40 hours of work by the student over the course of several months, outside of regular coursework
- a requirement of the Diploma Programme, which means it must be completed and passed for a student to be eligible for the Diploma

The extended essay aims to...

- foster student inquiry
- encourage intellectual and personal growth
- offer students the opportunity to engage in the high level research and writing they will see in college or university
- build transferable skills, knowledge and confidence for future projects
- help students develop confidence through accomplishment and satisfaction through the personal pursuit of knowledge
- help students make connections between coursework, their lives and our global society

The grade for the extended essay is combined with the student's theory of knowledge (TOK) grade to earn up to three points towards the IB Diploma, as shown in the following matrix.

		Extended essay				
		A	B	C	D	E or N
Theory of knowledge	A	3	3	2	2	Failing
	B	3	2	2	1	Failing
	C	2	2	1	0	Failing
	D	2	1	0	0	Failing
	E or N	Failing	Failing	Failing	Failing	Failing

The extended essay is a life-changing experience for students – one that resonates far beyond the project itself. It can be profoundly rewarding to mentor students during this pivotal moment in their academic and personal development.

Insights

'The EE totally changed the way I see myself and my studies. Before, I never really had the confidence to produce new knowledge on my own and didn't really think I had anything that real scholars would want to hear. Now I feel like I can take part in intellectual conversations about things I care about, and feel like I have found my voice!'

Sharon L., IB Diploma Programme graduate

The extended essay and the IB Diploma Programme

Throughout this handbook, you will see how the extended essay harnesses and strengthens elements of the IB learner profile and the Approaches to Learning skills (see pages 4–5).

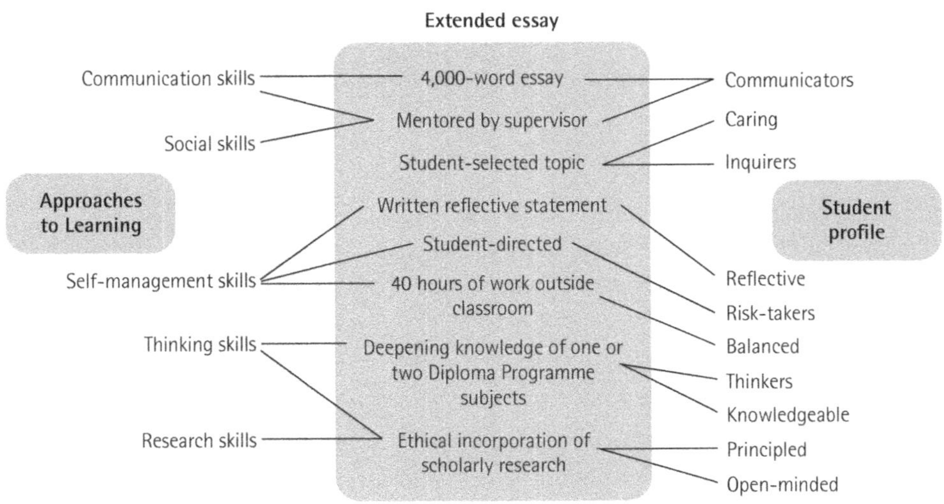

At the start of the process, it is also helpful to consider how the extended essay fits within the Diploma Programme as a whole.

The extended essay is part of the IB core:

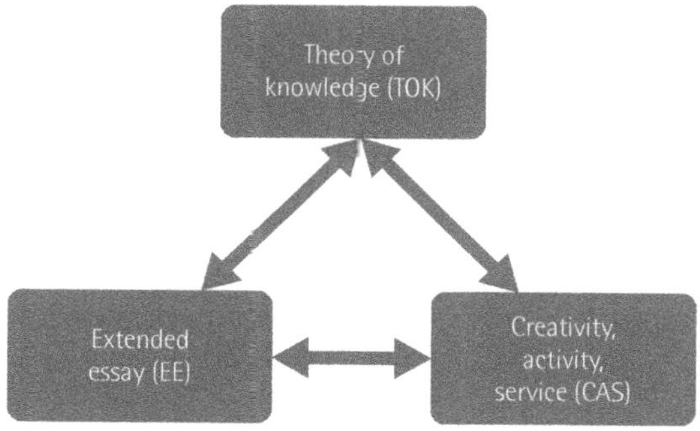

Like the learner profile and the Approaches to Learning, the core of the Diploma Programme is designed to develop the whole student – not just their academic and intellectual growth, but also their personal development as lifelong students and as global citizens committed to creating a more peaceful world.

How does the IB core, and the extended essay in particular, aim to achieve this development?

The three parts of the IB core work together to encourage inner reflection and outward engagement. That is, theory of knowledge, creativity, activity, service, and the extended essay help students become more aware of themselves (their beliefs and identities) as well as more aware of their contexts (local to global) and their ability to contribute to society.

Theory of knowledge (TOK):

- teaches students to think critically about the nature of knowledge
- offers space for **interdisciplinary** connections, differing perspectives and metacognition
- encourages awareness of the ethical considerations of systems of knowledge and truth.

Creativity, activity, service (CAS) offers students the opportunity to:

- explore new interests and abilities beyond academics
- develop collaborative, organisational and time-management skills
- realise the mutual benefits of service to others
- understand the importance of reflection and balance.

The extended essay (EE):

- reinforces the importance of reflection and metacognition
- further develops communication and time-management skills
- encourages connections between the local and the global
- allows students to strengthen thinking and research skills in a focused way, while enhancing knowledge and understanding of one or two IB Diploma Programme subjects.

These elements of the IB core help students become more aware of themselves – their interests, abilities, and values. They also build an understanding of how students belong to larger communities that can benefit from their insight, creativity, and compassion. In many ways, the extended essay is where students apply the skills and knowledge gained through theory of knowledge, CAS, and their Diploma courses.

Example

Mei, a Biology and Geography student, developed her extended essay around the research question: 'To what extent have local conservation efforts impacted butterfly biodiversity in urban parks within my city?'

Starting with theory of knowledge discussions about how scientific knowledge is constructed and verified, Mei applied this understanding to design a rigorous field research methodology. Her CAS experiences volunteering with an environmental group gave her practical context about conservation challenges and community engagement.

Through the extended essay process, Mei:

- reflected regularly with her supervisor on both successes and methodological challenges
- developed time-management skills balancing field work, data analysis and drafting
- connected her local findings to global butterfly conservation literature
- deepened her understanding of ecological sampling techniques from Biology while incorporating spatial analysis concepts from Geography.

Her supervisor noted that Mei transformed from a hesitant researcher to a confident scientist who could articulate complex relationships between human activity and biodiversity. After completing her essay, Mei presented her findings to the city parks department, demonstrating how academic research can contribute meaningfully to local communities, while addressing global environmental concerns.

This example shows how a student's extended essay experience:

- builds on knowledge from TOK and skills from CAS
- develops multiple Approaches to Learning skills
- connects local and global perspectives
- deepens subject-specific knowledge
- transforms students into more confident, skilled students
- has potential real-world impact.

The extended essay in the context of the IB assessment timeline

The extended essay is uniquely positioned in the IB Diploma Programme: it embodies the IB principle of 'concurrency of learning'. This key IB concept refers to the simultaneous study of diverse subjects throughout the two-year programme, allowing students to make meaningful connections across disciplines, rather than studying subjects in isolation. While the guide does not mandate specific start and end dates for the extended essay within the two-year programme (other than final upload dates), schools and colleges typically structure the process to allow students enough time for deep research and reflection. Most schools and colleges develop an internal timeline for the extended essay that allows:

- time for exploration of topics and development of research questions
- time for in-depth research and data collection
- opportunities for meaningful reflection throughout the process
- structured support through the three mandatory reflection sessions
- adequate time for drafting, revising and finalising the essay.

The extended essay exists alongside other assessment components, including internal assessments (IAs). While some IAs are completed within a single term or year, others – like the extended essay – may span both years of the programme. Schools and colleges carefully coordinate these assessment components to balance students' workloads.

The skills developed through the extended essay process – critical thinking, academic writing, research methods, time management, reflection – are transferable between other IB assessments. Students often find that progress in one area of assessment strengthens their approach to others, regardless of which they encounter first in the timeline. This interconnectedness of learning experiences is a cornerstone of IB philosophy.

As a supervisor or coordinator, understanding how the extended essay connects with other IB assessments can help you guide students to get the most out of each part, while keeping their overall workload manageable.

Reflection

Review the information about the learner profile and the Approaches to Learning on pages 4–5.

- Which Approaches to Learning skills and learner profile traits do you feel your teaching most often helps students develop?
- How might students transfer those skills and traits to the extended essay process, ultimately bringing those new strengths back to their study of your subject?
- How might the extended essay align with your original motivation for becoming an educator?
- What specific strengths from your teaching or administrative practice do you believe will serve you well as an extended essay supervisor or coordinator?
- When you think about the potential transformations students might undergo through the extended essay experience, which possibilities seem most significant or exciting to you?

Commitment to success

The extended essay can be a transformative experience for students *and* a rewarding experience for you. You can connect with individual students in a more informal setting, building positive and supportive working relationships outside the classroom or office. You will witness pivotal moments in students' lives as they gain new skills and confidence; and nurture 'inquiring, knowledgeable and caring young people who help to create a better and more peaceful world (International Baccalaureate 2025)'.

Key takeaways: Chapter 1

- The extended essay is a foundational component of the IB Diploma Programme core, combining independent research with guided supervision.
- As both a process and a product, the extended essay aims to develop students' research abilities, critical thinking skills and academic independence over approximately 40 hours of work.
- The extended essay works in tandem with theory of knowledge and CAS to develop reflective, knowledgeable global citizens who can make connections across disciplines.
- The extended essay contributes up to three points towards the IB Diploma (when combined with theory of knowledge), and is a required element for diploma eligibility.
- Supervising extended essays offers educators a unique opportunity to mentor students through academic research outside the traditional classroom environment.
- The extended essay process develops key attributes of the IB learner profile and strengthens all five categories of Approaches to Learning skills.
- As a component that embodies 'concurrency of learning', the extended essay allows students to deepen their knowledge in specific subject areas while making meaningful connections across the curriculum.
- The skills developed through the extended essay – including critical analysis, academic writing, time management, and reflection – are highly transferable to both university studies and future careers.

Key term

interdisciplinary: combining and integrating elements from two or more academic disciplines

2 Coordinator and supervisor responsibilities

This chapter covers the following:

- Key stakeholders and contributors in the extended essay process
- Coordinator responsibilities
- Supervisor responsibilities
- Student responsibilities
- IB requirements and recommendations

Key stakeholders and contributors in the extended essay process

The extended essay is successful when everyone involved understands their roles and responsibilities. That way, you can all work together to make the process efficient and meaningful.

Who is involved in the extended essay process?

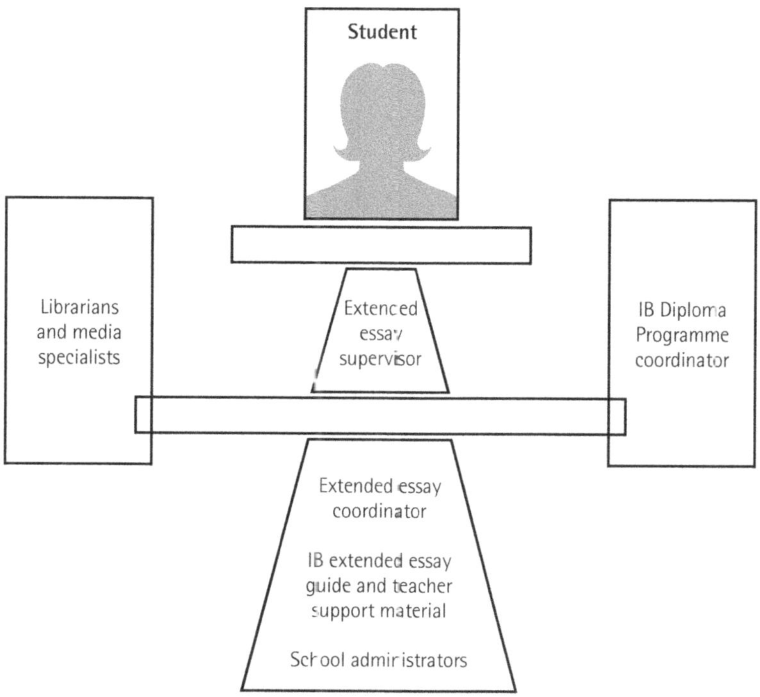

The diagram shows the student at the top of the extended essay structure, as the director of their own project. The extended essay supervisor is the student's main source of support and mentoring. In turn, the supervisor is usually supported by the extended essay coordinator, the IB Diploma Programme coordinator and other school administrators.

Additional support is provided by the IBO's own resources, such as the Extended essay guide (2025) and teacher support material, as well as the knowledge and expertise of media specialists and librarians at the school (see Chapter 9 for more on the importance of media specialists).

While the student is ultimately responsible for completing the extended essay, it is essential that both student and supervisor receive proper support throughout the process from other contributors. This includes dedicated time, training and mentoring of both students and less experienced supervisors.

Remember

Clear expectations and explicit student or professional development make all the difference. The more a student or supervisor knows, the more confident they will feel in meeting the demands of their respective tasks.

Strong IB programmes create a 'virtuous cycle' or 'positive feedback loop' where dedicated support for students cultivates academic success, which generates supervisor satisfaction and fulfilment. This satisfaction enhances programme quality and reputation, attracting and inspiring future students who perpetuate this cycle of excellence. Each component reinforces the others, creating an upward spiral of continuous improvement and achievement.

The virtuous cycle of strong IB programmes

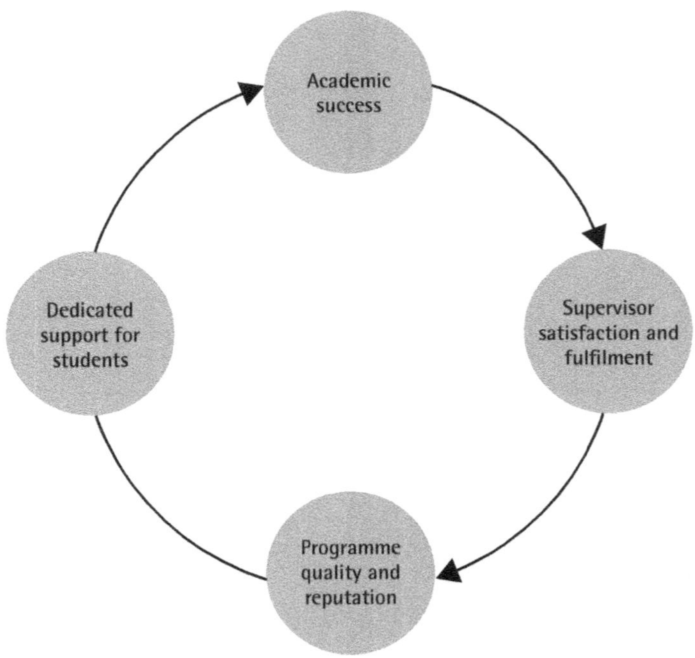

Coordinator responsibilities

Depending on the organisational structure of your school, roles may overlap. For example, the Diploma Programme coordinator may also be the extended essay coordinator, or another faculty member, such as a Diploma Programme subject teacher, or media specialist may be the extended essay coordinator. Whoever has this role, it is helpful to establish and maintain clear expectations regarding their responsibilities.

Extended essay coordinator responsibilities

Training and support

Extended essay coordinators should work closely with school administration to ensure that supervisors and students are adequately trained and equipped for the extended essay process. Such training may include:

- continuing professional development for teachers and supervisors, such as dedicated time to read and practise providing feedback or assessing sample student papers, or comparing predicted grades against assessed student work
- communication of subject reports and updates that may also impact extended essays in that subject
- offering new supervisors a more experienced mentor who can model supervisor meetings and answer questions that may arise
- ensuring that supervisors know how and where to access subject-specific guidance, sample papers and other material on the Programme Resource Centre (PRC) of the IBO website
- showing supervisors how best to mentor and support their students, as well as when to ask for help
- ensuring that supervisors are aware of both IB and school-determined processes, policies and ethical considerations.

Administrative duties

Administrative responsibilities include:

- ensuring that all extended essay materials satisfy the requirements as outlined in the IB's Diploma Programme assessment procedures
- pairing each student with a qualified supervisor – a member of staff at the school
- supporting supervisors as they authenticate student work
- abiding by the IBO's and the school's policies regarding academic integrity
- ensuring that all materials, including the essay and **reflection and progress form (RPF)** are submitted to the IBO by the appropriate deadlines
- working with stakeholders to create a schedule for the completion of the extended essay process.

Student support and education

Coordinators should:

- ensure that students receive instruction, training and other opportunities to maximise success on their extended essays
- explain to students and their families how the extended essay fits within the Diploma Programme as a whole, ensuring that they understand that the extended essay must be completed and passed with a grade of D or higher in order for the candidate to be eligible for the Diploma.

Communication and leadership

Extended essay coordinators also take a communication and leadership role that includes:

- communicating regularly with students, teachers, other faculty and staff, and student parents or guardians to ensure that everyone involved has the information and support they need to be successful
- helping all involved, especially students, teachers and supervisors, to remember how meaningful and transformative the extended essay process can be when approached with intention, enthusiasm and a positive mindset!

The value of subject reports

Subject reports are invaluable resources written by the principal examiner for each extended essay subject, who gather input from senior examiners, who in turn collect feedback from assistant examiners. These reports represent the collective voice of the examining team and provide a detailed analysis of trends in student performance, highlighting common strengths and weaknesses against each assessment criterion. Unlike generic guidance, subject reports offer subject-specific insights drawn from hundreds of actual essays assessed during each examination session.

Coordinators and supervisors should:

- access the most recent subject reports through the online PRC
- review the reports with supervisors during training sessions
- highlight key findings that relate to common challenges students face
- share relevant sections with students at strategic points in the process
- use the reports to inform the development of resources and workshops.

It is particularly effective to review specific sections of the reports with students, especially when they are drafting or revising their essays. For example, discussing the examiner's observations about Criterion C (Analysis and line of argument) can help students understand what constitutes effective analysis in their specific subject area. These insights from examiners who have evaluated hundreds of essays provide authentic guidance that can significantly improve student performance.

When sharing subject reports with students, consider creating simplified summaries that highlight the most relevant advice for their current stage in the process. This transforms examiner feedback into actionable guidance that helps students avoid common pitfalls and leverage successful approaches in their specific subject area.

Supervisor responsibilities

In brief the supervisor acts as a mentor, supporting the student in taking ownership of their extended essay. They are expected to understand the generic and subject-specific guidance, as well as the IB's extended essay guide. Throughout the process, the supervisor provides targeted support, including (but not limited to) the steps outlined below. For more detailed guidance, see Chapter 7.

Extended essay supervisor responsibilities

Guidance on research and writing

The supervisor should guide students in:

- refining the research question
- locating and evaluating appropriate sources
- reflecting on progress
- outlining, writing and revising
- ensuring academic integrity in the use of sources or AI tools
- identifying and working through obstacles and challenges
- accessing other sources of assistance, such as librarians or other subject-area experts.

Support and education

The extended essay supervisor ensures that students:

- have all materials they need, such as generic and subject-specific guidance or sample papers
- maintain academic integrity throughout, by reminding them to keep detailed records and to use proper citations, and by encouraging them to defend or discuss orally any part of their work.

Regular meetings and guiding reflection

Supervisors:

- meet with the student for the three mandatory check-in sessions (initial, interim and **viva voce**)
- meet with students at other times determined by the student and supervisor
- authenticate the student's final essay and **reflective statement**.

Example

Ms Chen, a History supervisor, demonstrates effective supervision through her structured, yet flexible approach.

During her initial meeting with Elisa, who was researching the economic impact of the Silk Road, Ms Chen noticed that Elisa's research question was too broad. Rather than simply telling her to narrow it, she asked, 'What specific aspect of the economic impact interests you most?' This prompted Elisa to consider geographic and temporal limitations.

For their interim meeting, Ms Chen prepared by reviewing Elisa's outline and research progress in advance. She observed that while Elisa had excellent primary sources on Chinese trade records, her essay lacked perspective from other regions. Ms Chen asked, 'Have you considered how we might find comparable records from Central Asian merchants?' This guidance helped Elisa develop a more balanced analysis.

Throughout the process, Ms Chen encouraged Elisa to maintain a research log. This not only created accountability but also provided a record of Elisa's growth, from a broad initial idea to a sophisticated historical analysis.

During the viva voce, Ms Chen began by asking Elisa to reflect on her journey: 'Looking back at where you started, what do you see as the most significant evolution in your thinking about this topic?' This open question allowed Elisa to articulate her intellectual growth before discussing specific aspects of her research.

This example reveals how a supervisor's approach should balance guidance with student ownership, create accountability while fostering independence, and emphasise reflection alongside academic rigour.

Student responsibilities

While this handbook is intended for the use of educators and administrators, it is important to reiterate that the extended essay is a student-directed project. To complete the process effectively, the student must take on several responsibilities, as shown below.

Student responsibilities

Take the initiative

- Adopt a proactive approach and take ownership of the process, rather than waiting for contact or deadlines from the supervisor or coordinator.
- Identify and call on internal motivation and desire for growth and improvement to make the most of the experience.

Plan and organise

- Create and maintain a realistic schedule based on the deadlines and guidance from the extended essay coordinator.
- Commit to spending about 40 hours on the project – ideally working two hours or more each week.
- Use the Researcher's Reflection Space (RRS) and other tools to keep research, notes, reflections and writing neat, clear and accessible.

Communicate with clarity and professionalism

- Be the primary communicator, reaching out in a timely manner to arrange supervisor meetings or ask for help.
- Take good notes during supervisor meetings, research and times of reflection.
- Practise professional communication skills, such as formal emails and academic writing.
- Attend meetings well prepared.
- Be open and honest with the supervisor.

Self-educate and ensure understanding

- Carefully read and ensure understanding of the generic guidance and subject-specific guidance for their selected extended essay subject (or two subjects, for an interdisciplinary essay).
- Ensure understanding of the nature of the interdisciplinary pathway, if applicable.
- Carefully read and ensure understanding of the assessment criteria, using it to inform the essay writing.
- Seek help, clarification and guidance from supervisor, coordinator, librarian or subject teacher, as needed.
- Ensure understanding of IB and school policies on academic integrity and ethical use of AI.

Document and reflect

- Keep detailed, regular records of work done, research notes and reflections to promote self-awareness, growth and to be able to produce a meaningful reflective statement at the end of the process.
- Record any use of AI tools.

Maintain academic integrity

- Carry out each part of the process with academic integrity.
- Give credit where credit is due.
- Submit the highest-quality work.
- Be honest about AI use.

The following chapters offer guidance for extended essay coordinators and supervisors on empowering and equipping students to be the leaders of this project.

Insights

'The EE was challenging because it was the first time I had to complete such a massive project mostly on my own. It was tough at first to keep a schedule, but I partnered with a friend, and we kept each other on track. Now I feel a lot more confident about working on my own and completing a big project. I think that'll help me in university and in my career.'

Donesh S., IB Diploma Programme candidate

IB requirements and recommendations

To promote success within the school and to maintain the integrity of the Diploma Programme, the IBO has established some general requirements that all stakeholders should be aware of. Extended essay coordinators should read all updates provided by the IBO to ensure they have the most recent guidance on regulations.

1 Supervision

Extended essay supervisors should be faculty members employed by the school. If a student also chooses to be mentored by someone outside the school, the school supervisor must still conduct the **reflection sessions** and sign the **reflection and progress form** (RPF). (There is more information on the regulations for external mentors in the extended essay guide.)

Each student must meet with their supervisor three times. These 'reflection sessions' must be recorded on the RPF. Students are encouraged to meet with their supervisor as often as both deem necessary, to nurture a meaningful relationship.

Supervisors will spend 3–5 hours with each student throughout the process – meeting with the student, reading the draft and final essay, and completing the RPF.

The supervisor must be able to authenticate the student's work – both the essay and the final **reflective statement**.

2 Documentation

All three reflection sessions (formal meetings with the supervisor) must be recorded on the RPF. The IB recommends the use of the **Researcher's Reflection Space (RRS)** as a tool for organising extended essay materials, such as research notes, drafts, reflections and citations.

3 Timing

Your school should establish a clear timeline of due dates and internal deadlines to frame the three required reflection meetings and the final submission due date. The extended essay coordinator – often working with the IB coordinator – typically communicates this timeline to students, and supervisors and should also establish key checkpoints throughout the process. These checkpoints help ensure that students and supervisors stay on schedule and allow for timely intervention if support is needed. (Planning and scheduling are discussed in more detail in Chapter 3.)

4 Academic integrity

Using the guidance from IB, your school should establish and uphold clear guidelines regarding academic integrity, such as the proper use of AI tools, accurate citation methods, and avoiding **collusion** or '**double-dipping**'. Supervisors should maintain an awareness of their student's work throughout the process, so that essays can be authenticated and any academic misconduct issues can be addressed immediately.

Supervisors are permitted to read and provide feedback on only one complete draft of the essay. They may not make any physical marks on or edit/correct the student's work

Supervisors play an important role in authenticating student work. The IB's scaffolded extended essay process provides natural checkpoints where supervisors can confirm the authenticity of student work through discussions, review of progress in the RRS, and observation of the student's developing ideas across multiple interactions. This process-based authentication is particularly valuable in the age of AI, where supervisors' familiarity with students' thinking and writing patterns becomes an essential component of maintaining academic integrity.

5 Submission

All extended essays and RPFs must be submitted to IB via the IB eCoursework system by the deadline issued by IB. Only authenticated student work should be submitted. The extended essay coordinator should ensure that files are no larger than 10 MB.

Reflection

Before beginning the process, give yourself time to reflect:

- How might you structure check-ins to track progress and celebrate small wins?
- How might you collect evidence of your supervisory practice to reflect on your own development as a mentor?
- How might collaboration between supervisors help to reflect, identify and share successful approaches to common extended essay challenges?
- What meaningful rituals or events could your school develop to mark key milestones in the extended essay process, acknowledging both student and supervisor efforts?
- How could you incorporate brief moments of reflection during supervisor meetings that help students connect their extended essay work to their broader academic and personal development?
- What framework might you create to help students recognise connections between their extended essay experience and future academic or professional pursuits?

Commitment to success

Whether you are an administrator or supervisor, you will find that clear and consistent communication with everyone reduces anxiety, increases engagement and makes the extended essay process more effective and meaningful. While led by the student, the extended essay is grounded in principles of collaboration, mutual care and balance – for students and adults alike!

Key takeaways: Chapter 2

- The extended essay process involves multiple stakeholders working together.
- Extended essay coordinators are responsible for supporting and training students and staff, pairing students with qualified supervisors, ensuring academic integrity, scheduling and planning, and maintaining communication among all stakeholders.
- Supervisors serve as mentors who guide students through the process, such as with research question development, source evaluation, reflection, and academic integrity, while conducting three mandatory check-in sessions.
- Students must take ownership of the process by proactively communicating with supervisors, understanding guidance materials, maintaining a realistic schedule, committing approximately 40 hours to the project, and upholding academic integrity.
- Clear IB requirements exist for supervision, documentation (including the RPF), timeline management, academic integrity practices, and submission protocols that all stakeholders must understand and follow.

Key terms

collusion: a violation of academic integrity, when two or more students work together on an assignment that is to be submitted for individual assessment, trying to submit work that is not completely their own

double-dipping: a violation of academic integrity, when a student attempts to submit material used for another IB assessment, such as part of the Biology IA for a Biology extended essay

reflection and progress form (RPF): records of the mandatory reflection sessions, the student's reflective statement and the supervisor's authentication of the student's work; the RPF is submitted to IB along with the student's essay; a template is available in the Programme Resource Centre of the IB website

reflection session: a formal conversation between the student and their supervisor, which takes place three times throughout the process; sessions are recorded in the RPF

reflective statement: a 500-word reflection written by the student after completion of the essay and viva voce, discussing and evaluating their experience during the extended essay process

Researcher's Reflection Space (RRS): a dedicated place for the student to keep all their extended essay materials, from sources to research notes to reflections; the RRS can be digital or on paper, or a combination of the two

viva voce: (Latin 'with living voice') the final session or 'interview' between supervisor and student, in which the student makes an oral defence of the extended essay after the supervisor has read it; this also includes discussion and reflection on the process as a whole and what the student has learned, personally and about the topic

3 Planning and timing

This chapter covers the following:

- Key deadlines and milestones in the extended essay process
- Supervisor meetings: formal and informal
- The benefits of explicit instruction and a structured approach
- Final submission timeline

Key deadlines and milestones in the extended essay process

The extended essay reflects about 40 hours of work for the student and should be conducted over an extended period during the Diploma Programme. The final submission deadline is set by the IB and is communicated to schools each year. Once this date is released, coordinators and other stakeholders can plan accordingly to ensure students have sufficient time to complete the process.

While there are mandatory reflection sessions for the supervisor and student at three key stages of the process, the rest of the timeline is at your discretion. When back-planning from the final deadline, keep in mind any other deadlines for the Diploma Programme that have been set by your school or the IB. Teachers and administrators should plan together to ensure a fair distribution of school-determined deadlines, such as internal assessments, to ensure students are not overwhelmed, but have a balanced and manageable assessment schedule.

Think of the extended essay process as three major phases. Within each phase, there will be a formal supervisor meeting and probably one or two check-in sessions.

Phase 1: Beginning the process and selecting a topic

IB suggested timeline: 1–2 months

Coordinator	Supervisor	Student
Introduce students to the extended essay. Share the extended essay guide and relevant parts of the support material with students (and supervisors, if not already done). Remind students of academic integrity (and the ethical use of AI) in the extended essay process. Match students with supervisors. Provide any necessary training or mentorship to supervisors.	Read or reread the extended essay guide and support material. Familiarise yourself with all student and supervisor deadlines.	Read and ensure understanding of all background information. Brainstorm topics and subjects. Consider which pathway to choose. Decide on a topic, and carefully read and ensure understanding of the subject(s) of the extended essay.

Suggested and required meetings for Phase 1:

- **Suggested** 'get to know you' meeting between student and supervisor, to discuss the process, establish some goals and discuss the student's ideas or selected topic. The student creates a research plan and schedule of self-imposed, additional deadlines as a follow-up.
- **Required** formal first meeting, to discuss the research question and next steps and establish a research plan. This meeting should be recorded on the RPF.
- **Suggested** check-in once the student has begun research, ensuring they are on the right track and have all the support and guidance they need. This may include refining the research question and discussing ethical research.

Phase 2: Project development

IB suggested timeline: 2–3 months

Coordinator	Supervisor	Student
Support supervisors and students as questions or challenges arise. Provide students with relevant materials for optional internal deadlines such as outlines or annotated bibliographies. Assist supervisors as needed (such as with struggling students). Communicate deadlines and other required steps to supervisors, students and other stakeholders.	Support students as needed. Read and discuss full rough draft.	Conduct background research and delve deeper into focused research. Possibly create an annotated bibliography, an outline and 'chunked' portions of the essay in preparation for writing the essay. Compose a full rough draft. Meet with supervisor about rough draft.

Suggested and required meetings for Phase 2:

- **Suggested** regular check-ins over the 2–3 months to discuss progress, research and writing.
- **Required** interim meeting once the student has begun to write. This meeting should be recorded on the RPF.
- **Suggested** check-in to discuss the rough draft and the student's plans for revision (if not done during interim meeting).

Phase 3: Completion of the process

IB suggested timeline: 1–2 months

Coordinator	Supervisor	Student
Support supervisors and students: provide information and training regarding viva voce, predicted grades and completion of the RPF. Communicate deadlines and other required steps to supervisors, students and any other stakeholders.	Support students as needed. Read final essay. Conduct viva voce. Authenticate student's work by completing RPF.	Revise rough draft. Submit final essay. Attend viva voce to discuss process and growth. Compose reflective statement on RPF.

One meeting for Phase 3:

- **Required** final meeting (viva voce) once the student has submitted the final essay and supervisor has read it.

> **Insights**
>
> 'I really liked getting to know my supervisor. We met several times while I was working on my essay – knowing I had a meeting coming up helped keep me on track, and he was really helpful when I was feeling stuck. He helped me talk through some frustrations and realise how I could move forward.'
>
> Alex M., IB Diploma Programme graduate

Supervisor meetings: formal and informal

The IB extended essay is structured around three formal, required supervisor meetings. But both student and supervisor will benefit from additional meetings.

Formal supervisor meetings and reflection sessions

A record of the three formal supervisor meetings should be made on the reflections and progress form (RPF). Each one should be followed by some reflection on the part of the student, which can be recorded in their Researcher's Reflection Space (RRS):

- Initial reflection session (within the first month or so of the process, as students brainstorm, do background research, decide on a topic and develop a research question)
- Interim reflection (during the research and writing phase)
- Final reflection (after the final essay has been submitted)

Informal meetings and check-ins

The three formal meetings are designed to underpin a strong working relationship, so a few less formal meetings are recommended as often as the student and supervisor or coordinator deem necessary. The table below gives an example of when these informal meetings might take place and their purpose.

When	Meeting purpose
After the extended essay process has been introduced to students by the coordinator but before students have selected a topic or subject(s)	• Discussion of the student's interests and possible areas for research (if supervisors have already been assigned).

Once a provisional research question has been developed	• Discussion of the research question and relevant subject(s), depending on the student's chosen pathway (if an earlier meeting already occurred). • Initial rapport-building and discussion of interests and research direction (if this is the first meeting). • Setting personal goals. • Planning a research timeline with self-imposed deadlines aligned with school and IB expectations. • Reflection on what the student is discovering about themselves or the topic.
Once the student has begun conducting background research	• Review of early findings and exploration of questions or challenges. • Discussion of methodology. • Evaluation of the overall essay plan. • Reflection on personal and academic insights gained so far.
Once the student has completed some writing (for example, an annotated bibliography, an outline or part of the draft)	• Discussion of the development of the argument and thinking. • Assessment of writing for academic purpose. • Ongoing reflection on learning and self-discovery.
Once the student has completed more writing – for example, the first 2,000 words.	• Further discussion of argument development and critical thinking. • Continued assessment of academic writing. • Reflection on personal growth and evolving understanding of the topic.

Example

Stephanie is a student athlete interested in sports medicine, who hopes to become a physical trainer one day. She devised a Sports, Exercise and Health Science research question that she was happy with: 'To what extent does a four-week dynamic stretching routine affect hamstring flexibility and sprint performance in high-school athletes aged 16–18?' However, she began to experience problems when trying to recruit and retain peers to take part in her experiment. She requested a meeting with her supervisor, Mr Gomez. He listened as Stephanie explained her frustrations and her fear that her extended essay was in jeopardy.

After a few minutes of chatting, Mr Gomez asked Stephanie how she might broaden her pool of potential participants. Stephanie realised that she could recruit athletes in a variety of sports. Mr Gomez asked Stephanie to envision what might keep students from sticking with the experiment for the duration. She realised that people's busy schedules meant that she might need to communicate more frequently with her peers, sending reminders and thank you messages, for example. During the conversation, Stephanie also decided to ask a few extra students to participate and they could serve as 'buffers' in case other students dropped out during the four-week period. Stephanie left the meeting with a renewed energy and purpose, and also realised the importance of communication in working with others when conducting experiments.

The benefits of explicit instruction and a structured approach

The three formal supervisor meetings and the final deadline form the basic infrastructure for the extended essay project. However, it is helpful to create a schedule that provides explicit instruction and internal deadlines to build a strong structure for the process. The diagram below shows some of the ways students benefit from explicit instructions when planning and writing their essay, such as how to locate and evaluate scholarly sources, methods of outlining and organising, and how to write analytically.

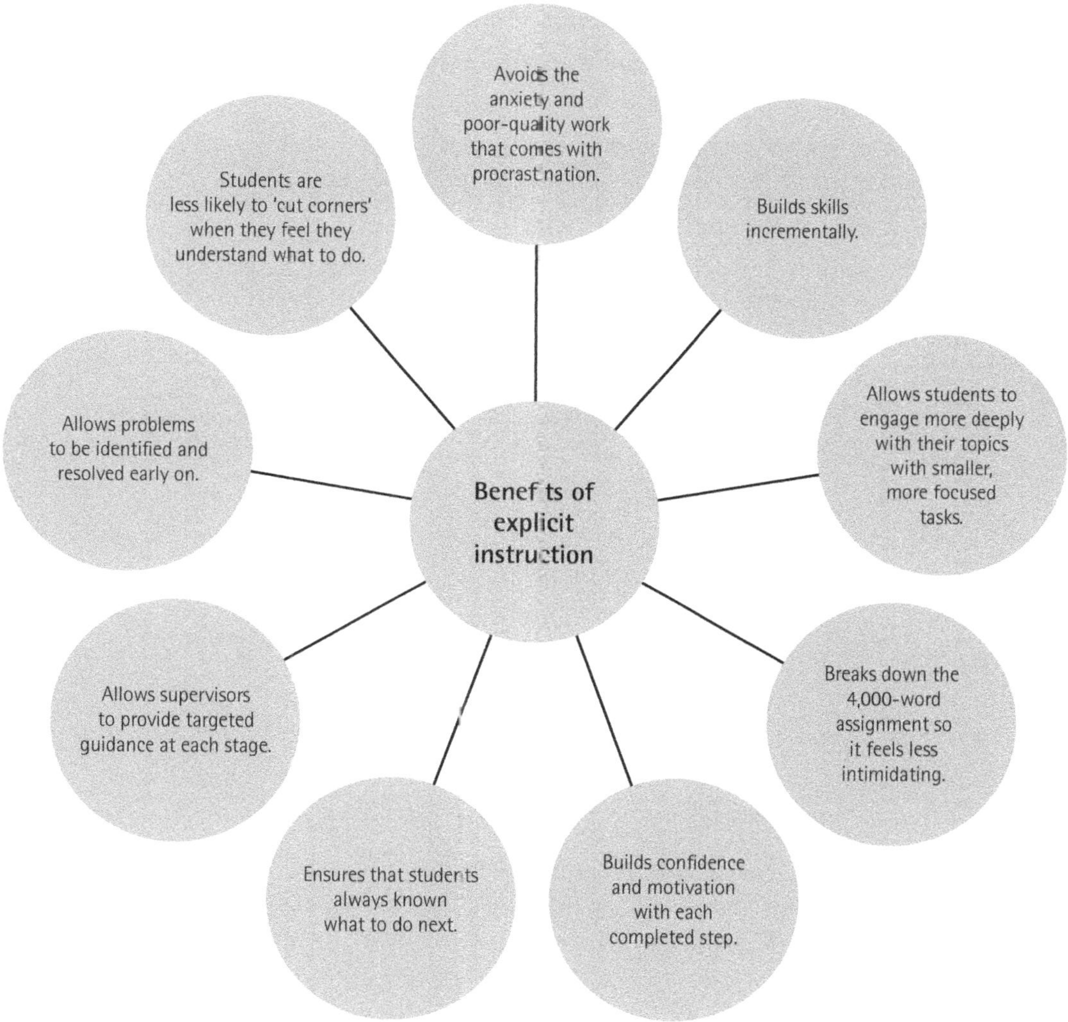

Insights

'As a teacher, I have found that my students tend to perform better when I break down complicated tasks into smaller steps and teach particular skills they will need for those steps. Many times I have thought a student was unwilling to complete an assignment, when really they were just unsure what to do and how to do it!'

Cecil L., IB Philosophy teacher

Explicit instruction and the Approaches to Learning

The extended essay draws on and helps develop a wide range of sub-skills and competencies within the IB Approaches to Learning:

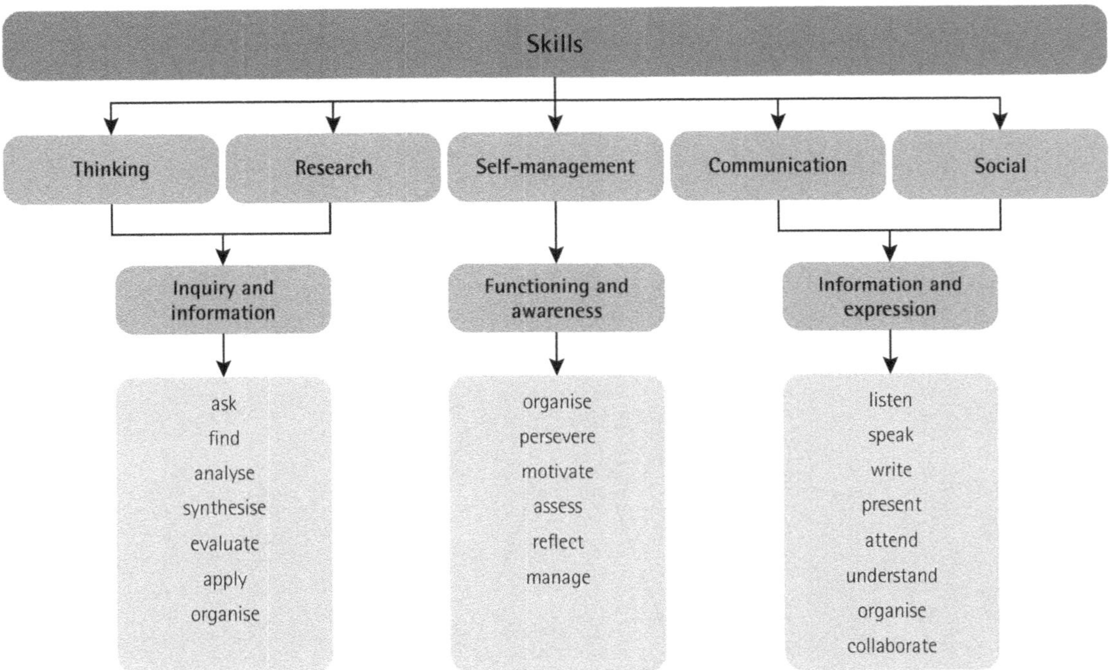

Many students will already possess the skills outlined in the flowchart, but they may not know how to apply them in a wide range of contexts. The information that follows provides some suggestions for how you can teach these skills as part of the extended essay process.

Thinking

- **Analyse research questions:** Use worksheets that break down example extended essay research questions to identify variables, scope and methodology.
- **Practice critical reading:** Create structured reading activities in which students identify claims, reasoning and evidence in academic articles.
- **Develop conceptual understanding:** Have students create concept maps linking their research question to broader theories and **frameworks** in their subject.
- **Encourage reflection:** Implement structured check-ins where students evaluate the effectiveness of their research methods and adjust accordingly.

Research

- **Teach information literacy:** Guide students in evaluating source credibility by creating a checklist (currency, relevance, authority, accuracy, purpose).
- **Model database searching:** Demonstrate **Boolean operators** and advanced search techniques in academic databases.
- **Scaffold note-taking:** Provide structured templates for annotated bibliographies that require students to summarise key points, identify methodology and note relevance to their research question.
- **Practise citation:** Hold workshops where students properly cite sources in their chosen format (MLA, APA, Chicago, etc.) with real examples from their research.

Self-management

- **Create detailed timelines:** Help students plan backwards from the final deadline with specific milestones and check-ins.
- **Teach project management:** Introduce tools such as **Gantt charts** or digital project boards for tracking extended essay progress.
- **Model productive work habits:** Demonstrate how to break large tasks into manageable chunks with specific examples.
- **Develop reflection habits:** Implement regular reflection prompts that are focused on process rather than just outcomes.

Communication

- **Structure academic writing:** Provide templates for different sections of the extended essay with sample paragraph structures; teach outlining.
- **Develop academic voice:** Analyse exemplar essays to identify formal academic language and tone.
- **Practise supervisor meetings:** Role-play effective conferences, focusing on asking specific questions and seeking targeted feedback.
- **Teach revision strategies:** Guide students through self-assessment using specific criteria from the extended essay assessment criteria.

Social

- **Facilitate expert interviews:** Teach students how to professionally approach and interview subject matter experts.
- **Encourage collaboration:** Create structured peer feedback sessions where students discuss and evaluate each other's topics and RQs.
- **Develop networking skills:** Guide students in reaching out to universities or professionals for specialised resources.
- **Practise academic discussions:** Hold seminars where students present and defend their extended essay proposals or research methodology to peers.

Remember

You may not include all the above when designing explicit instruction for your school's extended essay process. However, it helps if teachers and supervisors keep these skills in mind, encourage students to seek help when needed, and consider what resources and support the school can offer.

Reflection

Consider the following questions:

- How might I adapt the Approaches to Learning skills framework to address specific needs within my school's extended essay programme?
- Which areas of explicit instruction do my students typically need the most support with during the extended essay process?
- Which internal deadlines or checkpoints have been most effective in my experience, and which ones might I consider adding?
- How can I balance providing structure and guidance while still fostering student independence and ownership of the extended essay?
- What strategies have I found – or might I try – to help students develop self-management skills throughout the extended essay process?

Structured progression: Internal deadlines as scaffolding for academic success

Breaking the extended essay process into small, regular assignments and milestones helps students strengthen their Approaches to Learning skills and develop key IB learner profile traits. The information below shows a few ways that the extended essay process aligns with Approaches to Learning skills.

Self-management skills:

- A structured approach, with internal deadlines, helps students develop time-management and organisational skills.
- Staggered deadlines for components of larger projects teach planning and prioritisation.
- Self-assessment checkpoints encourage reflection on progress and process.

Research and thinking skills:

- Structured research assignments with clear expectations of source evaluation encourage students to develop critical assessment abilities and discernment of accurate information.
- Annotated bibliography requirements emphasise information literacy by promoting conscious reflection on source relevance, reliability and scholarly value.
- Explicit teaching of research methodologies enables students to understand and apply appropriate investigative approaches for different academic contexts.

Communication and social skills:

- Arranging and completing supervisor meetings requires students to communicate their questions, needs and goals clearly and effectively.
- Supervisor meetings offer practice in meeting with faculty or other professionals in a more formal setting.

The following chapters contain suggestions for scaffolding the extended essay process through explicit instruction and a clear structure, as well as other ways to support student success. However, many schools find it useful to implement the following structured approach, using internal deadlines, as part of that plan:

- Research question workshops
- Submission of formal proposal (including chosen pathway with justification; topic and research question with explanation and initial bibliography)
- Oral defence/discussion of proposal with supervisor or subject teacher
- Detailed, self-created research plan
- Initial, working bibliography or annotated bibliography (partial or full)
- Outline
- First 1,000 or 2,000 words
- Self-assessment of rough draft using assessment criteria
- Short reflections at different points in the process (to provide material for the reflective statement)

Final submission timeline

Extended essay coordinators should make sure there is enough time (at least one month) for the following key steps towards the end of the process:

- Student submits final extended essay.
- Supervisor reads final essay.
- Scheduling and completion of the viva voce.
- Student composes reflective statement.

Learner profile traits

- **Inquirers:** Assignments with inquiry-based components that require student-driven investigation foster curiosity and develop skills for independent research throughout life.
- **Knowledgeable:** Explicit connections between discipline-specific knowledge and its applications help students deepen their conceptual understanding and explore knowledge across a range of disciplines.
- **Principled:** Clear guidelines for academic integrity with opportunities to discuss ethical dilemmas strengthen students' commitment to honesty, fairness and respect for intellectual property.
- **Risk-takers:** Scaffolded challenges that push students beyond comfort zones with appropriate support encourage students to approach unfamiliar situations with courage and forethought.
- **Balanced:** Deadlines that account for workload across subjects and extracurricular commitments help students understand the importance of balancing different aspects of their lives to achieve overall well-being.
- **Reflective:** Structured reflection prompts throughout the process, not just at the end, encourage students to thoughtfully consider their own learning journey, strengths, and areas for growth while developing greater metacognitive awareness.

- Supervisor authenticates student's work and completes the RPF.
- Essay and RPF are uploaded to IBIS.

The time for (and between) each of these final steps will depend on your school's size, other deadlines, supervisor schedules, and so on. However, it is important to schedule adequate time in the final weeks to allow for the support of struggling students, supervisors' and coordinators' other commitments, and any unforeseen challenges or circumstances that may arise.

Example

Below is just one example of a timeline, but it is not intended to be prescriptive. Rather, this schedule provides general ideas for pacing. Your school may find that a more extended or condensed schedule fits your students' needs.

Month	Extended essay coordinator or supervisor	Student
1	Coordinator: • Introduce extended essay. • Review scholarly research and resources available in your school and community. • Review academic integrity; proper citation; ethical use of AI tools. • Conduct workshop on brainstorming and background reading. • Conduct workshop on using the RRS, time management, and maintaining balance. • Review the extended essay process with established supervisors; provide training/ mentoring for new supervisors. Supervisor: • Read/refresh knowledge of extended essay guide and teacher support material, relevant subject guidance/updates.	• Set up researcher's reflection space. • Read and ensure understanding of extended essay guide and other material provided by the school or the IBO. • Do background reading/ searching and brainstorm topics. • Workshop and refine topics and research questions. • Chat with subject teachers.
2	Coordinator: • Assign supervisors. • Act as support for supervisors and students as needed. Supervisor: • Meet and chat with students. • Set expectations and establish contract/ relationship. • Conduct first formal reflection meeting. • Act as support for student as needed.	• Meet with subject teacher(s) and/or supervisor (once assigned). • Continue background reading and initial research. • Draft research plan and set self-imposed deadlines. • Reflect on meeting(s) with supervisor.

Month	Extended essay coordinator or supervisor	Student
3	Coordinator: • Act as support for supervisors and students as needed. • Share past extended essays in subject(s) with supervisors and create time for reviewing sample papers and assessment criteria. Supervisor: • Act as support for student as needed. • Read a portion of student's draft (if not full draft). • Conduct second formal reflection session with student.	• Continue working (reading, researching, designing and conducting experiment or survey, gathering data, and so on). • Ensure continued and deeper understanding of selected subject(s)/determining integration of subjects (if following interdisciplinary pathway). • Reflect on meeting with supervisor. • Begin writing rough draft.
4–6	Coordinator: • Act as support for students and supervisors as needed. Supervisor: • Act as support for student as needed. • Read complete rough draft. • Meet with student about full draft.	• Finish writing rough draft. • Self-assess against assessment criteria. • Meet with supervisor to plan revisions. • Reflect on meeting.
7	Coordinator: • Act as support for students and supervisors as needed. Supervisor: • Act as support for student as needed.	• Revise rough draft.
8	Coordinator: • Act as support for students and supervisors as needed. Supervisor: • Act as support for student as needed. • Read final essay.	• Submit final essay.
9	Coordinator: • Act as support for students and supervisors as needed. • Celebrate success! Supervisor: • Conduct viva voce. • Authenticate student work and complete RPF.	• Participate in viva voce. • Write reflective statement. • Celebrate success!

Commitment to success

Thoughtful planning of this extended essay journey transforms what can be an overwhelming academic hurdle into a profound opportunity for growth. By providing structure, guidance and intentional reflection points, you will not only help your students complete a requirement, you will also cultivate skills of **metacognition** that will serve them throughout their academic career and beyond. When carefully structured, the extended essay process becomes a powerful vehicle for developing independent students who understand how to manage complex projects, think critically and reflect meaningfully on their own development – skills that transcend disciplines and prepare students for lifelong success.

Key takeaways: Chapter 3

- The extended essay process follows three major stages (topic selection, project development and completion) with three mandatory supervisor meetings that should be supported by informal check-ins.
- Breaking up the extended essay into smaller deadlines with targeted skill instruction helps students manage anxiety, build confidence and develop necessary academic competencies.
- The extended essay process naturally develops students' research, thinking, communication, social and self-management skills while cultivating key learner profile traits.
- Allow at least one month before the IB deadline for final submission steps, including viva voce, completion of the reflection statement and administrative requirements.

Key terms

Boolean operators: words or symbols such as 'and', 'not' and 'or', which are used to combine or exclude key words during an internet search in order to make the results more relevant and focused

frameworks: conceptual structures that organise thinking and provide contexts for understanding relationships between ideas

Gantt chart: a diagram or picture of the stages of a piece of work, showing stages that can be done at the same time and those that must be completed before others can begin

metacognition: knowledge and understanding of your own thinking, processes and approaches to a skill or task

4 Understanding the assessment criteria

This chapter covers the following:

- The role of assessment in the extended essay
- The assessment process
- Applying grade descriptors for predicted grades
- The assessment criteria (A–E)
- Connecting assessment to supervision practices
- Supporting students' understanding of assessment
- Teaching self-assessment

The role of assessment in the extended essay

As a supervisor or coordinator, you are not just guiding students through a research project, you are helping them develop skills that will serve them throughout their academic careers and beyond. Clearly understanding the assessment criteria will allow you to provide targeted guidance that helps students succeed. Think of assessment not just as the final evaluation of your students' work, but as a powerful teaching tool you can use throughout the extended essay process. When you understand what to look for, you can better guide your students at every stage – from choosing a topic to writing their conclusion.

Assessment as a teaching tool

The assessment criteria give you a clear framework by which to guide your students. The criteria break down the essential elements of high-quality academic research and writing into specific components that you can address in your supervision sessions. You should:

- use the criteria to structure your check-in meetings with students
- refer to them when giving feedback on drafts
- frame your questions to help students think about specific criteria
- help students identify gaps in their work before submission.

Your supervision impacts how well students perform against the assessment criteria. The following supervision–assessment cycle illustrates how targeted guidance at each stage supports students to meet specific criteria. Effective supervision creates a continuous feedback loop that enables students to recognise strengths, address weaknesses, and progressively improve the quality of their work against all assessment criteria.

The supervision–assessment cycle

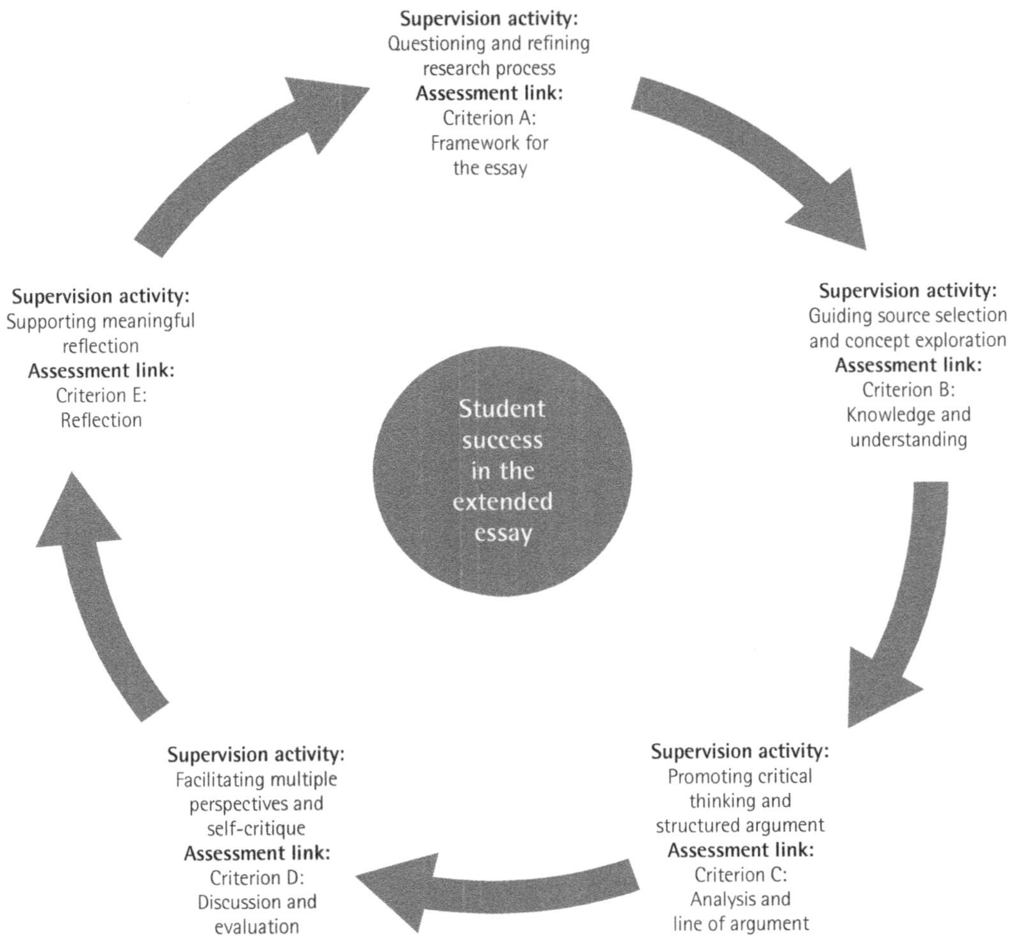

It is important to provide guidance without directing students' work. Understanding the assessment criteria will help you define this boundary. Think of yourself as a facilitator who helps students understand what is required and develop the skills to meet those requirements independently.

The assessment process

When you know how students' work will be evaluated, you can prepare them for success. So, it helps to understand this before approaching assessment.

There are two assessment frameworks, as shown in the table below.

Assessment criteria (A–E)	Grade descriptors (A–E)
Used by examiners for numerical marking	Used by supervisors for predicted grades
Detailed, specific indicators	Holistic descriptions of performance
Result in marks out of 30	Result in letter grades A–E
Five separate criteria (A–E)	Five grade levels (A–E)
Used throughout the extended essay process	Used primarily at the end of the process

While supervisors do not assign numerical scores, understanding how examiners apply a **best-fit approach** to the assessment criteria helps supervisors guide students and predict grades.

The best-fit approach acknowledges that student work rarely fits perfectly into a single level descriptor. Instead, examiners (and supervisors when predicting grades) look **holistically** at the essay and determine which level most accurately represents the overall quality of the work.

The key principles are:

- holistic judgement – looking at the complete picture rather than using a checklist
- positive approach – giving credit for what students have achieved rather than penalising what they have not achieved
- balance – weighing strengths against limitations to determine overall quality
- flexibility – recognising that excellence does not require perfection in every aspect.

Examiners apply this approach using the following process:

1. Read level descriptors starting from the highest level and working down.
2. Identify which level descriptor most appropriately describes the work.
3. If a piece seems to fall between two levels, reread both and choose the more appropriate one.
4. Within a level, award higher marks if the work demonstrates qualities to a greater extent.
5. It is not necessary for every indicator within a level to be met for that mark to be awarded.

Example

Imagine that a student's extended essay is being examined against Criterion A.

Aspect	Quality level
Research question	Clear, focused and relevant (Level 5–6)
Research methods	Mostly suitable but explained with partial effectiveness (Level 3–4)
Structure	Effectively supports communication (Level 5–6)

Best-fit thinking: Since two of three indicators match Level 5–6, but one important element only reaches Level 3–4, an examiner might award a mark of 5 (the lower end of the 5–6 band). This acknowledges the strengths while accounting for the less developed aspect.

Applying grade descriptors for predicted grades

As an extended essay supervisor, you will need to submit a predicted grade for each of your students. Predicted grades use the A–E grade descriptors rather than the detailed numerical criteria used by examiners.

Follow these steps to determine a predicted grade. Remember that grade descriptors are applied holistically – you are looking for the best overall match, not a perfect match on every point.

1 Read through the complete grade descriptors for all five levels (A–E).

↓

2 Read your student's completed essay, keeping the descriptors in mind.

↓

3 Determine which set of descriptors best matches the overall quality of the essay.

↓

4 Assign the corresponding letter grade as your prediction.

You might face some of the following challenges when assigning predicted grades:

- Overestimating performance: It is natural to be optimistic about your students' work; try to remain objective.
- Focusing too much on one criterion: Remember to consider all aspects of the essay, not just the ones that stand out.
- Confusing criteria and descriptors: Keep in mind that you are applying holistic grade descriptors, not detailed criteria.
- Subject-specific considerations: Some subjects may have expectations that affect what constitutes excellence.

To overcome these, discuss borderline cases with colleagues or your extended essay coordinator, and familiarise yourself with exemplar essays from your subject area.

Remember

When determining predicted grades, avoid the temptation to focus primarily on a student's writing style or presentation. A well-written essay with sophisticated vocabulary but lacking in analysis may score lower than a plainly written essay with excellent critical thinking. Remember that the grade descriptors emphasise analytical depth, coherent argumentation and critical evaluation more than stylistic elements.

The assessment criteria (A–E)

The extended essay is assessed against five criteria (A–E), with a total of 30 marks possible. Each criterion focuses on a different aspect of the essay, with specific indicators of quality at different performance levels.

Criterion	Focus	Maximum marks
A	Framework for the essay	6
B	Knowledge and understanding	6
C	Analysis and line of argument	6
D	Discussion and evaluation	8
E	Reflection	4
Total		**30**

The following information explores each criterion in detail to show you how you can guide your students towards success.

Criterion A: Framework for the essay (6 marks)

Guiding question: Do the research question, research methods and structural conventions followed provide an effective framework for the essay?

Criterion A assesses three key **strands**:

- Research question
- Research methods
- Structure

What to look for:

- Research question: The research question must demonstrate clarity, precision and relevance to the chosen field while remaining manageable within the essay's scope, serving as the explicit foundation that guides the entire investigation.
- Research methods: The methods should be clarified and suitable for answering the research question within the subject area
- Structure: Effective use of structural conventions that support communication of the research. This includes appropriate organisation, section headings, citations and presentation of visual materials.

You can guide your students in the following ways:

For research questions:

- help students refine overly broad questions into focused, manageable ones (see Chapter 5)
- encourage them to phrase questions to promote analysis rather than description
- guide them to check that their question aligns with subject-specific requirements.

For research methods:

- discuss which methods would be most appropriate for their specific research question
- prompt them to explain why they have chosen particular methods
- ensure they understand the ethical considerations related to their research methods.

For structure:

- introduce them to the structural conventions of academic writing in their subject
- share examples of well-structured essays in the subject area
- remind them that structure should enhance readability and support their argument.

Key questions to ask students:

- How does your research question invite analysis rather than description?
- What specific research methods will allow you to answer your question effectively?
- How will you organise your essay to guide the reader through your argument?

Insights

'I've found that spending extra time on the research question pays dividends throughout the entire process. When students truly understand what makes a good research question – specific, focused, analytical – they're already halfway to meeting Criterion A. I always tell new supervisors: if the foundation isn't solid, the whole structure becomes unstable.'

Marcela J., Extended Essay Coordinator with 12 years of experience

Criterion B: Knowledge and understanding (6 marks)

Guiding question: Does the student demonstrate knowledge and understanding of the subject matter being used in their research?

Criterion B assesses three key strands:

- Knowledge
- Understanding – Terminology
- Understanding – Concepts

What to look for:

- Knowledge: You should seek evidence that students have immersed themselves in comprehensive study of their subject, utilising high-quality, relevant source materials that directly inform their topic. Students' essays should demonstrate not just collection but thoughtful application of this research, showing they have built a solid foundation of knowledge that enables them to engage meaningfully with their specific research question.
- Understanding – Terminology: The effective use of subject vocabulary throughout an essay signals a student's grasp of their field's language. Rather than just sprinkling specialised terms randomly, look for consistent and precise application of terminology that naturally flows within the writing, demonstrating that students have internalised the professional discourse of their chosen subject area.
- Understanding – Concepts: Beyond basic facts, you should evaluate how well students explain and employ the underlying theoretical frameworks essential to their topic. A strong extended essay reveals students' ability to navigate key models, theories, and conceptual structures relevant to their research question, showing they can move beyond information gathering to genuine conceptual understanding.

You can guide your students in the following ways:

For knowledge:

- help them identify comprehensive and authoritative sources
- encourage them to find subject-specific academic sources
- guide them to evaluate the quality and relevance of their sources.

For terminology:

- review their work for accurate use of subject-specific terminology
- suggest resources that can help them understand key terms in their subject
- remind them to use terminology consistently throughout their essay.

For concepts:

- discuss the key concepts, theories or models relevant to their topic
- help them see connections between concepts and their research question
- encourage them to explain concepts in their own words rather than simply quoting sources.

Key questions to ask students:

- Which specific sources will give you the depth of knowledge you need for this topic?
- What are the essential terms someone would need to understand to follow your argument?
- How do the concepts you are using help answer your research question?

Criterion C: Analysis and line of argument (6 marks)

Guiding question: Does the student analyse the information presented in the essay and produce a coherent line of argument?

Criterion C assesses two key strands:

- Analysis
- Line of argument

What to look for:

- Analysis: Strong essays transform raw data into meaningful insights through thoughtful interpretation rather than mere description. Look for students who consistently dig beneath surface observations to uncover significant patterns and relationships within their research. This analytical approach allows students to extract relevant findings that contribute substantively to addressing their research question, revealing the deeper implications and significance of what they have discovered.
- Line of argument: Successful extended essays maintain a coherent thread that guides readers from research question through findings to well-reasoned conclusions. Rather than presenting disconnected information, students should craft a logical progression where each element builds upon previous points, creating a sustained narrative supported by compelling evidence. This connected argumentative structure demonstrates the student's ability to synthesise their research into a unified, purposeful response to their initial inquiry.

You can guide your students in the following ways.

For analysis:

- help them distinguish between description and analysis
- encourage them to ask 'why' and 'how' questions about their findings
- guide them to look for patterns, relationships and contradictions in their research.

For line of argument:

- discuss how to structure an argument that flows logically from start to finish
- help them see how each point they make should connect to their research question
- encourage them to signpost their argument with clear transitions and linking statements.

Remember

One of the most common issues in student essays is a disconnect between the research question and the line of argument. Many students conduct good research and include solid analysis but fail to explicitly connect their points back to their research question throughout the essay. This can significantly impact their performance.

In a strong line of argument:

- each major point clearly advances the response to the research question
- transitions between sections explicitly connect to the research question
- the reader can follow a logical path from research question to conclusion
- the essay feels purposeful and directed rather than meandering through information.

Common problems to watch for include:

- 'information dumping', where students include interesting facts without explaining their relevance
- sections that feel disconnected from the main inquiry
- a lack of signposting that shows how each section contributes to answering the research question
- a conclusion that introduces new ideas rather than synthesising previous arguments.

You can help students by:

- encouraging them to include a 'roadmap' in their introduction outlining how they will answer the question
- suggesting that they begin each major section by connecting it to the research question
- recommending they end each body paragraph by explaining how the point contributes to answering the research question
- getting them to practise articulating in one sentence how each section of their essay helps answer their research question.

The best essays maintain this thread from research question through analysis to conclusion, giving readers a clear sense of purpose and direction throughout.

Criterion D: Discussion and evaluation (8 marks)

Guiding question: Does the student discuss the findings and evaluate the essay?

Criterion D assesses two key strands:

- Discussion
- Evaluation

What to look for:

- Discussion: You should seek evidence that students can thoughtfully explore their findings from multiple angles, weighing different interpretations and contextualising results within broader implications. A successful discussion balances various perspectives on the research outcomes, supported throughout by specific evidence that substantiates each point of consideration rather than relying on unsupported assertions.
- Evaluation: The strongest essays demonstrate students' capacity for honest self-assessment, acknowledging both achievements and shortcomings in their work. Rather than presenting their research as flawless, students should critically examine the effectiveness of their methodological choices, identify limitations in their approach or data, and consider how these factors might have influenced their conclusions.

You can guide your students in the following ways:

For discussion:

- encourage them to consider different perspectives on their findings
- help them see the broader significance of their research
- guide them to support their discussion with specific evidence.

For evaluation:

- discuss the strengths and limitations of their research approach
- help them identify factors that might have affected their findings
- encourage honest self-assessment without undermining their overall argument.

Key questions to ask your students:

- What are the different ways to interpret these findings?
- What is the significance of what you have discovered?
- What are the strengths and limitations of your approach?

The difference between analysis and evaluation

Students often struggle to differentiate between the two essential skills of **analysis** (Criterion C) and **evaluation** (part of Criterion D), so it is important to help them understand the distinction.

Analysis involves	Evaluation involves
• breaking down information to examine component parts • interpreting findings and data • identifying patterns and relationships • explaining how evidence supports claims • developing a coherent line of argument.	• making judgements about the quality, value or significance of findings • considering strengths and limitations of research methods • weighing up different perspectives or interpretations • assessing the reliability and validity of evidence • considering wider implications.

Help your students move from one to the other by encouraging them to ask:

- Analysis: 'What does this information show? How do I interpret it?'
- Evaluation: 'How significant, reliable, or complete is this information? What are its limitations?'

Example

Consider a student writing an extended essay in Economics on the economic impact of tourism in a coastal community.

Analytical statement: 'The data shows that during the five-year period following the development of the beachfront resort, local employment rates increased by 18%, while average household income rose by 22%. This correlation supports economic theory regarding the multiplier effect, where direct tourism spending creates indirect benefits throughout the local economy through increased demand for goods and services.'

Evaluative statement: 'While the employment and income data indicate positive economic benefits from tourism, these figures must be assessed in context of several limitations. First, the benefits appear unevenly distributed, primarily benefiting property owners and hospitality workers, with minimal gains for those in traditional industries. Second, the seasonal nature of tourism employment creates economic vulnerability not captured in annual statistics. Third, the research methodology relies on official employment figures which may not account for informal economic activity that was displaced by tourism development.'

Now consider another example, from a student writing an extended essay in History on the causes of the French Revolution.

Analytical statement: 'The financial crisis of 1788 can be linked to France's involvement in the American Revolution. Financial records show that military expenditure increased by 250% between 1776 and 1783, while tax revenues remained stagnant due to aristocratic exemptions. This pattern reveals how foreign policy decisions directly impacted domestic financial stability.'

Evaluative statement: 'While financial factors clearly contributed to revolutionary conditions, judging their significance requires considering the limitations of focusing solely on economic causes. Contemporary pamphlets suggest that ideological factors may have been equally important, as Enlightenment ideas had been circulating among the educated classes for decades. Additionally, the reliability of royal financial records must be questioned, as the monarchy had incentives to misrepresent the true state of finances to various stakeholders.'

Notice how analysis identifies and interprets patterns in the evidence, while evaluation makes judgements about the significance, completeness, and limitations of that evidence.

Criterion E: Reflection (4 marks)

Guiding question: Does the student evaluate the effect of the extended essay learning experience on them as a student?

Criterion E applies only to the reflective statement on the student's reflection and progress form (RPF).

Criterion E assesses two key strands:

- Evaluative reflection
- Growth and transfer of learning

What to look for:

- Evaluative: Consistently evaluative reflection on the extended essay learning experience that includes specific examples. Students should go beyond description to analyse what they have learned.
- Growth: Consistent evidence of the student's growth and transfer of learning. Students should demonstrate how they've developed as students and how they might apply these lessons in the future.

You can guide your students in the following ways:

For evaluative reflection:

- help them distinguish between descriptive and evaluative reflection
- encourage them to include specific examples from their experience
- guide them to reflect on both successes and challenges.

For growth:

- discuss how they have grown as researchers and writers
- help them identify the transferable skills they have developed
- encourage them to think about how they might apply these skills in the future.

Key questions to ask students:

- How has this process changed you as a student?
- What specific skills have you developed that you will use in the future?
- How might you approach a similar project differently next time?

There is more information on how students can earn maximum marks in Criterion E in Chapter 8.

Connecting assessment criteria to supervision practices

Understanding the assessment criteria gives you a strong framework for structuring your supervision. Each criterion corresponds to different phases of the extended essay process and suggests specific approaches you can take to support your students.

The table below maps supervision activities to assessment criteria.

Criterion	Supervision phase	Key supervision activities
A: Framework	Early planning	• Helping develop focused research questions • Guiding selection of appropriate methods • Discussing effective essay structure
B: Knowledge and understanding	Research	• Suggesting quality sources • Discussing key concepts and terminology • Checking depth of understanding
C: Analysis and line of argument	Developing the draft	• Encouraging analytical rather than descriptive writing • Helping students develop a coherent argument • Suggesting ways to link ideas logically

D: Discussion and evaluation	Later drafting stages	• Prompting consideration of multiple perspectives • Encouraging critical evaluation of research • Discussing strengths and limitations
E: Reflection	Throughout, especially in reflection sessions	• Facilitating meaningful reflection • Helping students articulate learning and growth • Discussing transfer of skills to future contexts

By aligning your supervision activities with specific criteria, you can provide targeted support that helps your students excel in each area of assessment.

Insights

'I like to think of the assessment criteria as a roadmap for my supervision. When a student is struggling, I can usually trace it back to a specific criterion that needs attention. For example, if their draft is mostly descriptive, we need to work on Criterion C. If their sources are limited, we focus on Criterion B. This approach lets me give targeted guidance rather than overwhelming them with general feedback.'

Rafael K., Extended Essay Supervisor

Supporting students' understanding of assessment

One of your most important tasks as a supervisor is to help students understand the assessment criteria. When students internalise what they should be aiming for, they can take greater ownership of their work and make more informed decisions. There are several ways in which you can support students in this understanding.

Introduce assessment early

Do not wait until the final stages to discuss assessment with your students. Introduce the criteria early in the process.

- Share simplified versions of the criteria in your first meetings.
- Explain how each criterion relates to different aspects of the research and writing process.
- Revisit the criteria at key milestones to help students self-assess their progress.

Make assessment accessible

The formal language of assessment criteria can be intimidating for students. Help make it accessible.

- Translate criteria into student-friendly language.
- Create checklists based on the criteria that students can use throughout the process.
- Use concrete examples to illustrate what success looks like for each criterion.

Using exemplars

Exemplar essays can help students understand the assessment criteria in action.

- Share excerpts from sample essays that demonstrate excellence in specific criteria.
- Discuss what makes these examples effective.
- Encourage students to identify strengths and weaknesses in the samples.

The IB provides subject-specific exemplar essays that include marking comments so that students can understand how assessment criteria are applied. These materials can be accessed on the IB Programme Resource Centre.

Teaching self-assessment

One of the most valuable skills you can help your students develop is evaluating their own work against the assessment criteria. When students can identify their own strengths and areas for improvement, they take ownership of their learning and develop critical metacognitive skills.

There are various approaches you can take to teaching self-assessment.

1 Translate criteria into accessible language

Help students understand assessment expectations by rephrasing official criteria in more accessible, student-friendly language. For example, 'analysis' can be explained as 'explaining why your evidence matters', and 'evaluation' as 'judging the strengths and limitations of your findings'.

2 Create opportunities for guided practice

Before students assess their own work, provide opportunities to practise applying criteria to sample excerpts. This low-stakes practice builds confidence and clarifies expectations.

3 Introduce simple self-assessment techniques

Rather than complex rubrics, teach students straightforward methods they can apply independently, such as the colour-coding technique. This is an effective method that helps students visually identify the presence or absence of key elements in their work. You can introduce it in the following way.

- Explain the colour-code system by having students use four different colours to highlight key components: one for claims and arguments, one for evidence and examples, one for analysis (explaining the significance of evidence), and one for evaluation (assessing reliability, limitations, or significance).
- Ask students to check for balance by reviewing their highlighted text to see if all four colours appear in appropriate proportions. Essays with little or no analysis or evaluation often score lower on Criteria C and D.
- Help students connect their highlighted work to assessment criteria by showing how analysis supports Criterion C and how evaluation relates to Criterion D. Sparse use of the relevant colours can reveal areas needing improvement.

The self-assessment cycle

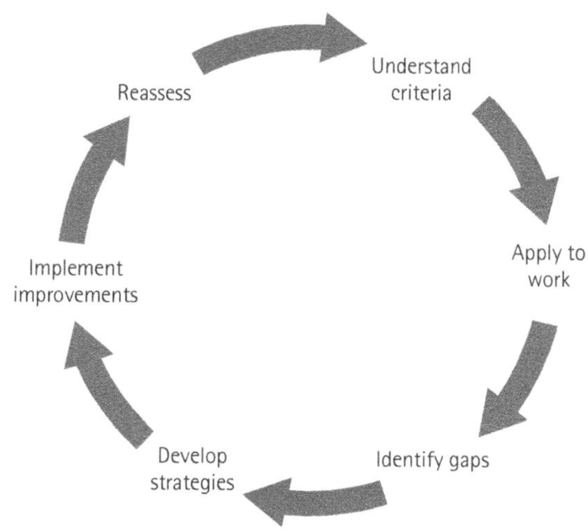

- Use the colour patterns to guide revision strategies. For example, if there is evidence without analysis, students should explain why that evidence matters. If analysis is present but lacks evaluation, they should assess the limitations or wider implications.

This visual approach makes abstract assessment concepts concrete and helps students identify specific areas for improvement. As a supervisor, you can use this technique during check-in meetings to illustrate how their work aligns with assessment expectations.

Key questions to guide student self-assessment

When helping students evaluate their own work, consider providing prompts for each criterion.

Criterion A (Framework)

- 'Is your research question clearly stated in the introduction?'
- 'Have you explained your research methods and why they're appropriate?'

Criterion B (Knowledge)

- Have you demonstrated depth of knowledge about your topic?
- Are subject-specific terms used accurately throughout?

Criterion C (Analysis)

- Do you explain the significance of your evidence?
- Is there a clear thread of argument linking your points?

Criterion D (Discussion)

- Have you considered different perspectives on your findings?
- Are the strengths and limitations of your approach addressed?

Criterion E (Reflection)

- Does your reflection include specific examples from your experience?
- Have you identified transferable skills you have developed?

By focusing on **criterion-referenced** questions, you will give students valuable guidance that helps them develop their own critical assessment skills.

Remember

Share these key messages with students:

- Excellence ≠ Perfection: The highest-level descriptors do not require faultless performance.
- Strengths can offset weaknesses: Strong performance in some areas can partially compensate for limitations in others.
- Major weaknesses matter: Significant problems in core areas will affect the overall assessment level.
- Self-assessment is valuable: Understanding the criteria helps students identify their own areas for improvement.
- Focused revision is effective: Prioritise improving aspects that might be pulling down the overall assessment.

Reflection

Take some time to consider how you might apply the assessment criteria in your supervision practice. Ask yourself these questions:

- How might I incorporate discussion of specific assessment criteria into my regular check-in meetings with students?
- What strategies could I develop to help students distinguish between descriptive writing and the analytical writing required for Criteria C and D?
- Which assessment criterion do I feel most confident explaining to students, and which might require more of my attention or professional development?
- How could I use exemplar essays or sample excerpts more effectively to illustrate what excellence looks like for each criterion?
- In what ways might I adapt my feedback style to better align with the assessment criteria while still maintaining student ownership of the work?
- What specific techniques could I implement to help students develop meaningful self-assessment skills they can transfer to other academic contexts?

Commitment to success

Assessment is not just about measuring achievement – it is also about defining and communicating what excellence looks like. When you understand the assessment criteria, you transform from someone who simply supervises to someone who guides with precision and purpose. Your insight into what makes an outstanding essay becomes the compass that helps your students navigate their journey. By making the invisible visible – through clear, supportive assessment conversations – you empower your students far beyond the extended essay.

Key takeaways: Chapter 4

- The assessment criteria provide a valuable framework, not only for evaluation but also for guiding the entire extended essay process.
- Each criterion focuses on a specific aspect of the essay: framework (A), knowledge and understanding (B), analysis and line of argument (C), discussion and evaluation (D) and reflection (E).
- Understanding how examiners apply the criteria using a best-fit approach helps you provide more effective guidance.
- When predicting grades, use the holistic A–E grade descriptors rather than the detailed assessment criteria.
- Helping students understand and internalise the assessment criteria empowers them to take ownership of their work and make informed decisions.

Key terms

analysis: the process of breaking down information to examine relationships between elements, interpreting findings, identifying patterns, and explaining how evidence supports claims within a line of argument

best-fit approach: an assessment method where examiners determine which level descriptor most closely matches the quality of the student's work overall, recognising that not all aspects may perfectly fit a single level

criterion-referenced: An assessment approach that evaluates student work against established standards or criteria rather than comparing it to other students' performance

evaluation: making judgments about the quality, value or significance of findings, considering strengths and limitations, weighing different perspectives and assessing the reliability and validity of evidence

holistically: considering all parts of something together rather than focusing on individual elements in isolation; in assessment, examining the complete work and how elements interact rather than evaluating separate components independently

strand: a specific element or component within an assessment criterion that examiners evaluate; each criterion typically contains two or three strands that together determine the overall quality for that criterion

5 Guiding students in topic and pathway selection

This chapter covers the following:

- The supervisor's role in topic selection
- Supporting the student's decision-making process
- Guiding students through pathway selection
- Strategies for effective supervision of interdisciplinary essays

The supervisor's role in topic selection

Your main role during topic selection and refinement of the research question is to facilitate, question and mentor – not to prescribe or determine. The extended essay is designed to be student-driven, and students should maintain ownership throughout their research journey. However, your knowledge and professional judgement will be key to helping students navigate what may be their first significant independent research project.

Your mentorship at this initial stage will lay the groundwork for the entire extended essay process. Without directing students toward specific topics or questions, you can still support them by helping them to:

- evaluate whether their interests can evolve into a manageable research question
- refine working research questions
- assess the accessibility of resources for potential topics
- understand the boundaries of a 4,000-word academic essay
- recognise how their ideas align with subject frameworks
- determine whether their ideas promote analytical thinking rather than mere description.

Insights

'I've found that my most rewarding supervision experiences happen when I resist the temptation to suggest topics and instead help students discover their own path. When students genuinely connect with their research question from day one, they typically remain motivated even during the inevitable challenging phases of research and writing.'

Priya M., Extended Essay Supervisor, Biology

Finding the balance: guidance versus direction

One of the most nuanced aspects of supervision is striking a balance between offering guidance and directing – or controlling – the process. The following table highlights effective approaches that maintain this delicate balance.

Do ...	Don't ...
✓ pose thought-provoking questions that encourage deeper consideration	✗ provide ready-made topics or research questions
✓ support students in exploring diverse possibilities before committing	✗ direct students towards areas that align with your own interests rather than theirs
✓ assist students in assessing how realistic their ideas are	✗ dismiss ideas without exploring their potential value
✓ direct students towards valuable research resources	✗ conduct the preliminary research on the student's behalf
✓ discuss the elements of effective research questions	✗ formulate or extensively rewrite their research question for them
✓ guide students on appropriate use of AI tools for idea generation.	✗ allow AI to determine or write their research question.

Reflection

Think about your approach to guiding students in previous academic projects. Ask yourself: When have I provided too much structure or too little support? What impact did that have on student engagement and ownership? How might I adjust my supervision style to better empower students while still offering the guidance they need?

Supporting the student's decision-making process

At the start of the extended essay journey, students need to identify areas of genuine interest – something that many find challenging. The Student Handbook contains ideas for independent brainstorming activities, but you can enhance their exploration through guided discussions.

Structured brainstorming activities

There are also several techniques you can try to support students in systematically exploring interests and transforming them into viable research questions.

Interest mapping

Ask students to spend 6–7 minutes writing freely about topics they find intriguing, then ask them to identify and mark recurring themes or concepts that emerge. Guide them to cluster related ideas and to identify patterns, then help them to connect these clusters to specific Diploma Programme subject areas. Discuss how these connected ideas might form the basis of potential research questions.

Remember

If students mention using AI tools for brainstorming, remind them that – while these can provide initial ideas to consider – the final research question must be their own creation.

Weighted topic evaluation

Another helpful tool is a type of **decision matrix** – a weighted evaluation matrix that helps students systematically assess multiple potential topics.

Example

When Marc met with his supervisor for their first session, he was considering three potential topics: ecological succession in abandoned urban areas (Biology), sustainable urban planning for flood-prone coastal cities (Geography), and agricultural adaptation strategies in response to climate change (ESS).

His supervisor suggested creating an evaluation matrix to help him make a more informed decision. Together, they developed criteria and weighted them according to importance on a scale of 1 to 5.

Criteria (weight)	**Urban ecology (Biology)**	**Sustainable urban planning (Geography)**	**Agricultural adaptation (ESS)**
Personal interest (x 3)	4 (12)	3 (9)	5 (15)
Research feasibility (x 2)	3 (6)	4 (8)	4 (8)
Analytical potential (x 3)	4 (12)	5 (15)	3 (9)
Resource availability (x 1)	3 (3)	5 (5)	4 (4)
Connection to future aspirations (x 2)	2 (4)	3 (6)	5 (10)
Weighted total	**37**	**43**	**46**

This systematic approach helped Marc realise that, while all three topics had merit, he was most passionate about agricultural adaptation strategies, and this topic also connected most strongly with his interest in pursuing sustainable agriculture after graduation.

Guiding preliminary research

After students have identified potential topics, they need to carry out some initial explorations to determine their viability. Your guidance during this phase is essential for developing effective research habits. This is also an excellent time to call on librarians and media specialists (see Chapter 9).

Consider offering students:

- suggestions for specialised academic databases relevant to their subject area
- frameworks for evaluating source reliability and relevance
- tutorials on constructing effective search queries with appropriate keywords
- templates for documenting initial findings in their Researcher's Reflection Space (RRS)
- guidelines for ethical use of digital research tools, including AI assistance (there is more detailed guidance on research methods in Chapter 6).

Remember

Encourage students to document not only what they discover during their preliminary research, but also what they struggle to find. Significant gaps in available information can either indicate an opportunity for original investigation or suggest that a topic may be too narrow or underdeveloped for a substantial extended essay.

From topic to research question

Many students find transitioning from a general area of interest to a focused, analytical research question challenging. You can facilitate this process through a structured questioning sequence.

The research question development funnel:
Moving from a broad interest to a focused, analytical research question

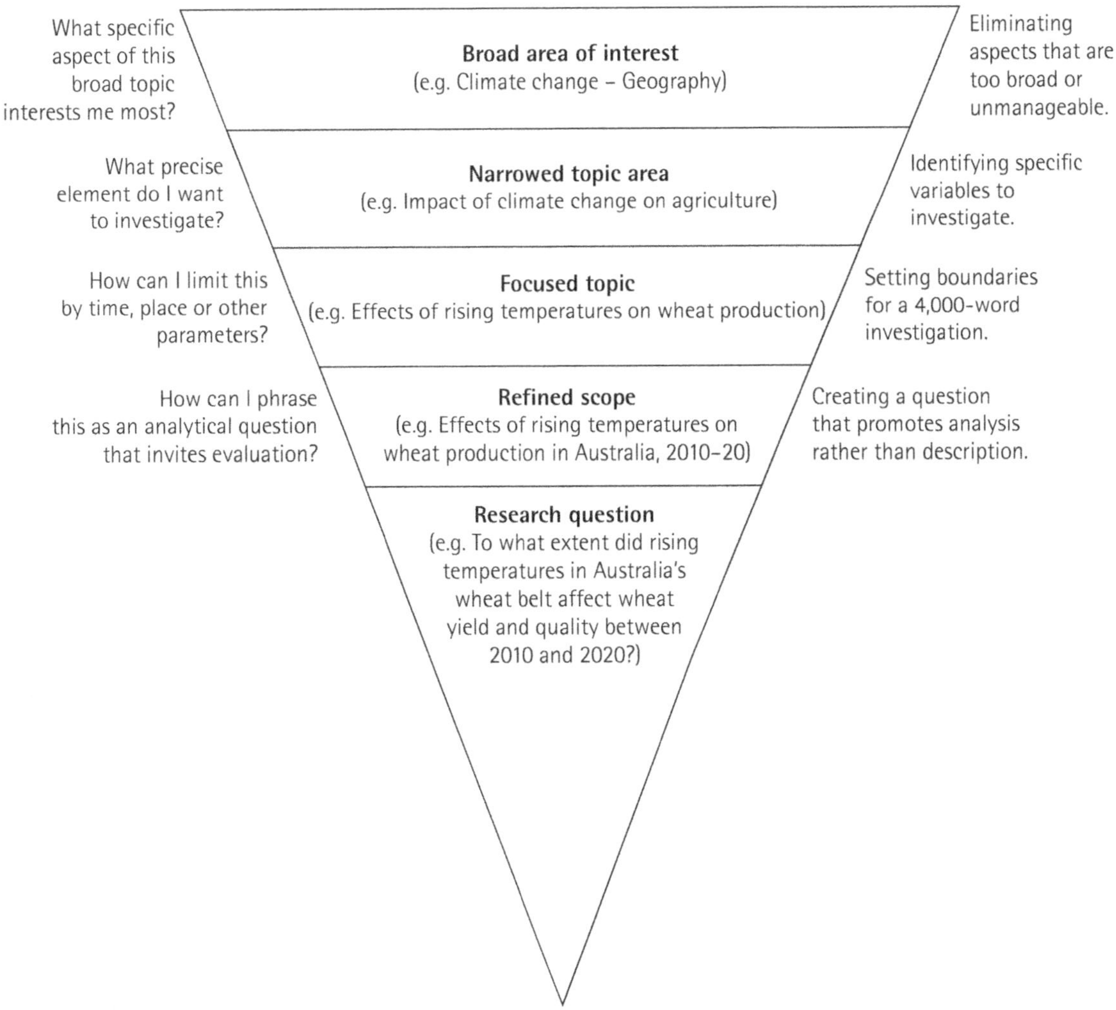

Example

Consider these examples of topic refinement.

Overly general → appropriately focused

- Initial topic (Environmental Systems and Societies): 'Renewable energy'.
- First refinement: 'Solar energy implementation'.
- Further refinement: 'Residential solar panel adoption'.
- Additional focus: 'Factors influencing residential solar panel adoption in suburban communities'.
- Research question: 'To what extent do financial incentives versus environmental concerns drive residential solar panel adoption in suburban Phoenix, Arizona (2015–2023)?'

Overly general → appropriately focused

- Initial topic (Language A): 'The use of sound in Shakespeare's plays'.
- First refinement: 'Sound devices in Shakespeare's *Hamlet* (1623)'.
- Further development: 'Shakespeare's use of sound devices to reinforce themes in *Hamlet* (1623)'.
- Final research question: 'How does Shakespeare use sound devices to comment on the relationship between speech, power and truth in *Hamlet* (1623)?'

Remember

When guiding students on their research question, remember that questions beginning with 'How' or 'To what extent' typically lead to more analytical responses than those beginning with 'What' or 'When'. A well-crafted research question should be narrow enough to be manageable within 4,000 words but complex enough to sustain a substantive discussion. The research question is the compass that guides the entire essay – investing time in refining it early will save hours of revision later.

Guiding students through pathway selection

A crucial decision all students have to make is whether to pursue the **subject-focused pathway** or interdisciplinary pathway. Your role is to help them understand what each entails without imposing your own preference. The following table can be used to guide students in making the decision that is right for them.

Subject-focused pathway	**Key decision factors**	**Interdisciplinary pathway**
Explores a topic through one Diploma Programme subject lens.	**Research question**	Integrates knowledge from two Diploma Programme subjects.
When the question can be fully answered using theories, methodologies and concepts from a single subject.	**When does it work well?**	When the question exists at the intersection of subjects and requires multiple perspectives.

Builds on existing knowledge in a subject already being studied.	**Subject knowledge**	Requires foundational knowledge in both subjects (it is recommended students study at least one of them in the Diploma Programme).
Uses established methodologies from a single discipline.	**Research methods**	May require combining or adapting methodologies from both disciplines.
Allows for deeper exploration within one knowledge domain.	**Depth vs. breadth**	Enables broader exploration across knowledge domains, while still requiring depth.
Typically has clearer boundaries and expectations.	**Structure**	May require more creative structuring to effectively integrate both subjects.
May be more manageable for first-time researchers.	**Complexity**	Can be more challenging but potentially more rewarding.
'To what extent did Nazi propaganda influence German youth between 1933 and 1939?' (History)	**Example**	'How do economic incentives and psychological factors interact to influence environmental conservation behaviour?' (Economics and Psychology)

Encourage students to ask themselves the following questions.

- Does my genuine interest lie primarily within one subject area?
- Would bringing in a second subject significantly enhance my understanding?
- Am I comfortable working within the frameworks of both subjects?
- Does my topic naturally bridge two subjects?
- Which approach will best allow me to develop a meaningful analytical argument?

Remind them that the decision should be based on which approach best serves their research interests and question, not which one might be easier or more impressive.

Subject-specific pathway

The **subject-specific pathway** allows students to explore a topic within the boundaries of a single Diploma Programme subject. This approach offers several benefits; it:

- leverages and deepens existing subject knowledge
- permits in-depth analysis within established disciplinary frameworks
- typically offers well-defined methodological approaches
- may be more manageable for students with developing research skills.

If students are considering this pathway, encourage them to:

- consult the subject-specific guidance in the extended essay materials
- explore how their interests connect to fundamental concepts within the subject
- identify relevant theories, models or methodologies from the subject
- consider whether their topic can be thoroughly examined through one disciplinary lens.

Example

Javier approached his supervisor with an interest in exploring how memory functions during high-stress situations. His initial thoughts encompassed psychological theories, neuroscience research and even evolutionary biology perspectives.

His supervisor asked, 'Which aspect of memory and stress most intrigues you?' and Javier explained that he was particularly curious about how stress affects memory during academic testing situations.

Rather than suggesting that Javier pursue multiple disciplinary angles, his supervisor helped him explore how psychological theories and research methods could provide a comprehensive framework for investigation. They discussed cognitive load theory, test anxiety research and experimental methodologies in psychology.

Through this conversation, Javier developed a focused research question within Psychology: 'To what extent does test anxiety impair working memory function in adolescents during timed assessments?' This approach allowed Javier to conduct more in-depth analysis within psychological frameworks rather than attempting to integrate multiple disciplines within the constraints of the extended essay format.

Interdisciplinary pathway

The interdisciplinary pathway enables students to investigate topics that benefit from integrating two Diploma Programme subjects. This approach also offers several benefits; it:

- allows exploration of complex issues that exist at disciplinary intersections
- promotes innovative connections between knowledge domains
- creates opportunities for original analysis and perspectives
- reflects how many significant real-world challenges require interdisciplinary thinking.

If students are considering this pathway, help them to:

- understand the five interdisciplinary frameworks provided by the IB:
  - power, equality, justice
  - culture, identity, expression
  - movement, time, space
  - evidence, measurement, innovation
  - sustainability, development, change
- determine whether their topic genuinely benefits from combining disciplines
- identify how theories, methods and concepts from both subjects will meaningfully integrate
- anticipate the challenges of synthesising different disciplinary perspectives.

Remember

The interdisciplinary pathway requires genuine integration of two subjects, not simply including content from both. Help students understand that successful interdisciplinary work synthesises perspectives to create insights that neither discipline could achieve alone.

Strategies for effective supervision of interdisciplinary essays

Supervising an interdisciplinary extended essay presents unique challenges, especially when your expertise may be limited to only one of the disciplines involved. Some effective support strategies are outlined below.

Acknowledging expertise boundaries

Be transparent about the limits of your knowledge. Remind students that the extended essay is student-directed, which means that ultimately they are responsible for ensuring they know and understand a subject or subjects.

Navigating interdisciplinary supervision

If a student combines subjects that are both beyond your specialisation:

- openly acknowledge your areas of expertise and knowledge gaps
- facilitate connections with colleagues who have relevant subject expertise
- direct students to official subject-specific resources
- focus on guiding research methodology and argumentation rather than specific content knowledge.

When you have expertise in one subject area:

- guide students confidently in your area while being honest about limitations in the other subject area
- help students identify methodological approaches from your subject area
- arrange consultations with colleagues who have expertise in the complementary subject
- focus on helping students articulate how the two disciplines enhance each other
- ask questions that prompt students to explain concepts from both fields clearly.

When you have limited expertise in both subject areas:

- emphasise research skills, academic writing conventions, and critical thinking
- help students break down complex questions into manageable components
- guide students in finding authoritative resources in both disciplines
- schedule occasional meetings with subject specialists for content guidance
- focus on the logical structure and coherence of the student's argument.

Facilitating interdisciplinary integration

One of your most important roles when supervising an interdisciplinary essay is helping students genuinely synthesise two disciplines rather than treating them separately. Consider these approaches:

- Identify shared concepts: Help students recognise concepts that appear in both disciplines, potentially with different meanings or applications.
- Explore complementary methodologies: Guide students in understanding how research methods from different disciplines can work together.
- Focus on integration points: Encourage students to identify specific aspects of their topic where the two disciplines must be combined for full understanding.

Example

Sofia wanted to explore the relationship between science-fiction literature and real scientific development, specifically how authors such as Isaac Asimov and Arthur C. Clarke anticipated and potentially influenced real technological innovations. Her supervisor had a background in literature but limited knowledge of physics and computer science.

Instead of attempting to guide Sofia on technical scientific concepts beyond her expertise, the supervisor:

- helped Sofia identify specific science-fiction works that made notable technological predictions
- arranged for Sofia to consult with a physics teacher about the scientific accuracy of various predictions in these works
- guided Sofia in developing a methodology that combined literary analysis (examining narrative techniques, themes and character development) with historical analysis of scientific development
- helped Sofia select 'evidence, measurement, innovation' as the most appropriate framework for her interdisciplinary essay
- encouraged Sofia to create a timeline comparing publication dates of key science-fiction works with the development of related technologies

The resulting essay effectively integrated literary analysis with scientific history, examining how fictional narratives may have inspired or reflected scientific innovation, despite the supervisor's limited expertise in one of the subjects.

Topic development questioning guide

Create a questioning framework to help students assess and develop their topic ideas before your meeting or check-in. Include prompts such as:

- What specifically fascinates you about this topic?
- How does this topic connect to key concepts in your chosen subject(s)?
- What aspect of this topic remains unclear or contested in the field?
- What types of primary and secondary sources would be relevant to this topic?
- What potential obstacles might you encounter in researching this topic?
- What methodological approaches would be appropriate for investigating this question?
- Which theories or frameworks from your subject(s) might help analyse this topic?
- How will this topic allow you to develop an argument rather than simply describe information?

Use their responses to guide your discussion.

Supporting students with decision challenges

Some students struggle to select a topic because they have too many interests or are concerned about making the 'wrong' choice. When working with these students:

- establish clear decision points and create a definitive timeline for narrowing options and final topic selection
- apply practical filters by evaluating options based on concrete factors like resource availability and methodological feasibility

- implement exploration periods by encouraging brief preliminary investigation of two or three top choices before committing
- emphasise skill development by reminding them that the research process builds valuable transferable skills regardless of topic
- address perfectionism by helping them understand that a 'perfect' topic is less important than one that is manageable, interesting, and analytically rich.

Reflection

As you prepare to guide students through the topic and pathway selection process, take a moment to consider:

- how you can help students identify which pathway – subject-focused or interdisciplinary – best aligns with their genuine intellectual curiosities rather than what they think might impress others
- times when you have seen students demonstrate deep disciplinary thinking or meaningful cross-disciplinary connections – how can you help them recognise these strengths in themselves as they consider their pathway choice?
- how you can draw upon students' experiences in their DP courses to help them recognise where their strengths might lie – whether in the focused application of one discipline or in connecting ideas across disciplines
- your own experiences with disciplinary and interdisciplinary thinking – how might sharing appropriate examples help students understand the value of both approaches?
- how to encourage students to be risk-takers in their chosen pathway – whether by diving deeper into disciplinary complexities or by exploring connections between subjects.

Commitment to success

The topic selection phase lays the foundation for everything that follows in the extended essay process. By providing thoughtful guidance while preserving student autonomy, you help develop the critical thinking and independent decision-making skills that extend far beyond this single assignment. Remember that your greatest contribution is not in crafting the perfect research question, but in nurturing students' ability to identify meaningful questions and develop the confidence to pursue them independently. This delicate balance between support and autonomy transforms the extended essay from a requirement into a truly formative educational experience.

Key takeaways: Chapter 5

- Your role as supervisor is to facilitate and guide rather than direct. Students must maintain ownership of topic selection and research direction for their extended essay to fulfill its educational purpose.
- Effective guidance during topic selection involves asking thoughtful questions, helping students assess feasibility and directing them to appropriate resources, rather than providing ready-made answers.
- When helping students choose between subject-focused and interdisciplinary pathways, focus on which approach would best address their research interests and questions.
- For interdisciplinary essays, emphasise the importance of genuine integration rather than parallel treatment of two subjects. Help students identify where and how the disciplines can enhance each other.
- Be transparent about your expertise limitations when supervising interdisciplinary essays, and connect students with subject specialists when appropriate.
- Establish clear expectations about your supervisory role, meeting frequency and communication norms at the beginning of the process to avoid misunderstandings later.
- Guide students on the appropriate use of AI tools during topic selection, ensuring they understand that while these tools can assist with brainstorming, the final research question must be their own.

Key terms

decision matrix: an analytical tool that evaluates options against multiple criteria to enable systematic decision-making

subject-specific pathway: an approach that explores a topic through the lens and methodologies of a single academic discipline

6 Subject-specific guidance

This chapter covers the following:

- Subject-specific requirements: The importance of student knowledge and understanding
- Subject-specific guidance
- Combining subjects in an interdisciplinary extended essay

Subject-specific requirements: The importance of student knowledge and understanding

A key aspect of subject-specific requirements is the importance of student knowledge and understanding. Regardless of which pathway a student ends up selecting, their success will rely in large part on their knowledge and understanding of the theories, frameworks, concepts and methods of their chosen subject(s). Moreover, students may be writing on a subject with which a supervisor is less familiar, especially in the case of the interdisciplinary pathway. As such, it is vital that students can define and explain what constitutes knowledge and evidence in their chosen subject(s), as well as how research and data collection are done in these areas. Coordinators and supervisors should remind students to review not only the materials and knowledge from the Diploma Programme course itself, but also the subject-specific extended essay guidance for each subject in which they are interested.

Remember

Remind students that the extended essay is a self-directed process. It is *their* responsibility – not yours as supervisor – to know and understand the requirements of an extended essay in that subject(s). If they need more guidance or support, direct them to faculty and staff with the necessary knowledge.

Subject-specific guidance

Below are overviews of the six IB subject groups. Within these groups there are often several individual subjects, each with its own distinct requirements, expectations and considerations.

Language A

(Studies in Language and Literature)

An extended essay in Language A (the primary language in which the student is completing the IB Diploma):

- engages in literary and/or rhetorical criticism by analysing one or more texts
- discusses the author or authors' structural and stylistic choices (including literary and/or rhetorical devices and techniques) and the meaning they create
- uses existing scholarship and/or critical theory to shape and inform the analysis.

Requirements and specifications

- A Language A extended essay must focus on at least one text or work originally written in that language.
- It can explore a single text in depth or perform a comparative analysis of more than one work.
- It can focus on either literature or a language text.
- It may pair the work with a work or works read in translation for a comparative study.
- The focus of the essay should be on the literary or language text and not a social, philosophical or political issue. This means that a student may discuss a real-life issue such as a theme (say, the search for identity) but their discussion must remain grounded in the text, and should analyse how that real-life issue is portrayed in the work using various literary, rhetorical, structural and stylistic techniques.
- Students should avoid texts that are of questionable literary merit, and/or texts that do not have an established body of criticism. They might also consider pairing a less canonical text with a more traditionally 'literary' work.
- If their text is a film, they must discuss the screenplay just as they would the script of a play, and include consideration of visual, auditory and other non-verbal elements.
- Their essay must make use of both primary (the works under exploration) and secondary (literary criticism and scholarly research) sources.
- They may not use a work that they have studied in your Language A course, although they may select a different work by the same author.
- If they choose to compare two works, they should make clear why pairing these works for analysis enriches an understanding and appreciation of them both.

Sample topics

(Using English as the language A)

- 'How do Audre Lorde's poetry collection *The Black Unicorn* (1978) and Bhanu Kapil's *The Vertical Interrogation of Strangers* (2001) explore the role of hair as a symbol of cultural identity and assimilation in immigrant and diasporic narratives?'
- 'How has TikTok's algorithmic promotion of AAVE (African American Vernacular English) influenced its adoption and transformation among non-Black Gen Z users from 2020 to 2024?'
- 'How do Patrick Süskind's *Perfume* (1985) and George Orwell's *Animal Farm* (1945) use the manipulation of sensory experience as a metaphor for political control?'

Language B

(Language Acquisition)

An extended essay in Language B:

- offers students an opportunity to strengthen and enrich their fluency in, and knowledge of, the second language they are studying in your IB Diploma Programme and the culture(s) associated with that language
- can focus on either a literary work in that language, an aspect of the culture, the use of the language itself or a combination of these.

Requirements and specifications

- The text or texts being studied must have originally been written in Language B.
- If they choose the screenplay of a film, they should focus on the language rather than any cinematographic techniques or elements.
- If they choose to analyse texts, they should select ones (even non-traditional texts) that have a range of secondary sources associated with them.
- Their essay must make use of both primary (the works under exploration) and secondary (literary/cultural criticism and scholarly research) sources.
- In addition to their primary source(s), most of their secondary sources (if not all) should also be written in the target language.
- If they will be studying a culture associated with the language, they must:
  - focus on a social or cultural issue that is unique to the language
  - explore the topic as it influences the use or form of the language *or* explore the topic using some form of cultural evidence (or '**artefact**') such as a concrete object like a literary or creative work.

Sample topics

- (Translated from Language B: Spanish into the language of this handbook) 'How has the rise of voice-activated assistants like Alexa and Siri influenced the adaptation of Spanish command forms and politeness markers in Mexico?'
- (Translated from Language B: German into the language of this handbook) 'How does Patrick Süskind's *Das Parfum* use the motif of scent and olfactory imagery to represent the protagonist's isolation from and manipulation of society?'
- (For an IB Diploma candidate for whom Language B is English) 'How did Barack Obama's use of anaphora and parallel structure in his major speeches from 2004 to 2008 reflect and reinforce themes of national unity?'

Individuals and Societies

(Including Business Management, Digital Society, Economics, Geography, Global Politics, History, Philosophy, Psychology, Social and Cultural Anthropology, and World Religions)

An extended essay in an Individuals and Societies subject:

- offers the chance to explore a topic related to the human experience
- offers a multitude of perspectives and frameworks through which to select a topic
- can explore a topic of current global interest or an issue from another time or place.

Requirements and specifications

- Most Individuals and Societies extended essays require a combination of primary and secondary sources *except* Psychology and Social and Cultural Anthropology:
  - An extended essay in Social and Cultural Anthropology will need to rely primarily on existing ethnographic studies and on secondary sources (unlike the IA, which is based mainly on students' own fieldwork and other primary sources).
  - An extended essay in Psychology must be based on secondary sources (such as existing studies) only (unlike the IA in Psychology, which requires them to replicate an existing study and gather their own primary data).

- Because there are so many subjects within the Individuals and Societies category, it is very important for students to ensure they know and understand the specifics of their selected subject, including their subject's guidelines on what constitutes appropriate primary and secondary sources, data, evidence and theories.
- Remind students to carefully read the subject-specific guidance and the course syllabus on their selected subject (or subjects, in an Interdisciplinary essay) – especially if they do not yet have a deep understanding of the subject.

Sample topics

- (Digital Society) 'To what extent have IoT-enabled smart classrooms enhanced elementary student mathematics learning outcomes in the United States?'
- (Global Politics) 'To what extent has the 2023 Willow Project approval transformed environmental policy priorities and Indigenous consultation processes in United States Arctic governance?'
- (Interdisciplinary, combining Philosophy and Economics) 'To what extent does the rise of algorithmic decision-making in financial markets challenge traditional concepts of moral responsibility and market rationality?'

Insights

'One year, we did not have enough History extended essays for all of us History teachers to supervise, so I ended up guiding one student in a Social and Cultural Anthropology extended essay and another in Psychology. At first, I was hesitant as I didn't feel as confident in the methods and terminology of those subjects, even though they're also Group 3 subjects. However, after reading through the syllabuses and subject reports for both courses and chatting with some colleagues, I actually learned as much as my students! I now have a better understanding of both of those subjects, both how they differ from History as well as what we share.'

Polly B., IB History teacher

The Sciences

(Including Biology, Chemistry, Computer Science, Design Technology, Physics, and Sports, Exercise and Health Science)

An extended essay in a Sciences subject:

- investigates a scientific research question by gathering primary or secondary data through experimentation
- must make a valid conclusion based on sound evidence
- relies on scientific method
- is the only instance in which students are allowed to collect experimental data for their extended essay.

Requirements and specifications

- A science extended essay can take a variety of approaches. It may be:
  - based on raw data (either the student's own or the raw or processed data of another source, analysed by the student)
  - based on an experiment that they design and perform

  - undertaken using a theoretical approach, in which they create, test and analyse a model
  - a quantitative or qualitative analysis of a larger phenomenon, using a survey
  - a combination of any of the above.
- If a student wishes to conduct an experiment, they should ensure it can be completed in the time and resources available to them.
- An experiment should be conducted under the supervision of a teacher at the school.
- It should use the International System of Units (SI).
- It is not necessarily a problem if the results of their experiment do not prove their hypothesis: both negative and positive results are useful in their discussion and evaluation.
- If they are conducting an experiment that involves human subjects (such as in Sports, Exercise and Health Sciences), they must follow all guidelines and regulations set out by the IB regarding informed consent, ethical considerations and confidentiality requirements. Students are not permitted to perform any experiment on humans or animals that might cause anxiety, pain or any risk for the participants. A full explanation of these guidelines can be found on the IB website.

Sample topics

- (Biology) 'How does exposure to common household plant pathogens affect the growth and defence response of garden tomatoes (*Solanum lycopersicum*), as measured by visible symptoms and plant growth parameters?'
- (Sports, Exercise and Health Science) 'How accurate are wrist-worn fitness trackers in measuring heart rate compared to traditional chest strap monitors during different types of exercise intensities?'
- (Design Technology) 'To what extent has the transition from aluminium to carbon-fibre frames affected racing bicycle performance metrics in professional road cycling from 2010 to 2024?'

Mathematics

An extended essay in Mathematics:

- can be theoretical (focusing on 'pure' mathematical concepts, proofs, and abstract thinking) or practical (applying mathematical concepts to real-world questions or problems) or a combination of both
- offers the opportunity to apply mathematics to a topic of interest to the student
- may be shorter than the usual 4,000 words because of the large amount of algebra included in the essay.

Requirements and specifications

- For more theoretical essays, research will involve reading and selecting key secondary sources related to the theory.
- Students should ensure they are comfortable with the mathematics theory or concept they will be using and make clear that understanding in their introduction.
- For practical essays, the approach should be driven by the data but also flexible: students should avoid specifying mathematical or statistical methods in their research question. They may only determine the best analytical techniques after they have examined their data thoroughly. The research process thus might involve learning and explaining mathematical concepts that were not in their original plan but proved necessary based on what the data revealed.
- The strength of the essay lies in how effectively a student applies mathematical concepts to analyse their data and address their research question, not necessarily in the complexity of the mathematics used.

- It is best to use raw data that the student then analyses, rather than data that has already been processed by someone else (for example, rather than working with, say, published unemployment rates, students should gather their own data).

Sample topics

- 'How do variations in the complex quadratic polynomial $z^2 + c$ affect the boundary properties of the Mandelbrot set, and what mathematical patterns emerge from these variations?'
- 'How effectively can statistical methods identify and quantify the relationship between daily temperature fluctuations and local electricity consumption?'
- 'Using location optimisation theory, what is the most efficient distribution of emergency response units in Toulouse, France to minimise average response time based on historical emergency call data?'

The Arts

(Including Dance, Theatre, Visual Arts, Film and Music)

An extended essay in an Arts subject:

- can investigate a wide range of creative products and practices
- explores how the arts reflect the human experience
- should be based on an analysis of primary sources (the works of art themselves) in tandem with secondary, scholarly resources.

Requirements and specifications

- If students are writing on visual arts, dance or music, their essay should include sufficient primary sources to sustain meaningful and thorough analysis (for example, more than one sculpture or painting).
- Students should ensure they are comfortable with the methods of analysis of their selected subject, as well as the appropriate terminology.
- They should also make sure that their topic is focused on the artistic creation itself. This means that they may discuss a real-life issue, such as a theme (say, the loss of innocence) or a socio-political issue explored by the works, but their primary concern is to explore how the artist conveys this idea using the creative techniques available to them. Students should avoid topics that:
  - focus primarily on the artist's biography
  - attempt to prove one artist's influence on another
  - are more historical review of an artistic movement or artist than a close-reading of art pieces
  - focus on song lyrics or the social/historical evolution of a type of music – instead, they should analyse the music *as* music, discussing structure, style and technical elements.

Sample topics

- (Dance) 'How have African dance elements been integrated and transformed in Alvin Ailey's major works, particularly in *Revelations* (1960) and *Cry* (1971)?'
- (Theatre) 'How did Bertolt Brecht's alienation effect revolutionise audience engagement in political theatre, as demonstrated in *Mother Courage and Her Children* and *The Caucasian Chalk Circle*?'
- (Film) 'How did Satyajit Ray's use of naturalistic lighting and on-location shooting in *Pather Panchali* (1955) challenge the studio-bound conventions of 1950s Indian cinema?'

Cross-disciplinary subjects

(Including Environmental Systems and Societies, and Literature and Performance)

Although Environmental Systems and Societies and Literature and Film each integrate more than one discipline, IB classifies these subjects as 'cross-disciplinary' and single subject-focused. Because they are already interdisciplinary by nature, it is best not to combine either of them with a separate subject, as this would widen the topic beyond the scope of the extended essay.

Requirements and specifications

An Environmental Systems and Societies extended essay offers the opportunity to explore an environmental topic by examining it through the methods and theories of the humanities, such as economics, geography and other fields of human society.

There are many possible topics for an essay on ESS, but the focus should be on the interaction between humans and the natural environment.

Sample topics

- 'How do household income and ethnicity influence participation rates in recycling programmes across different Singapore neighbourhoods, particularly examining the effectiveness of blue bin initiatives?'
- 'To what extent is Brazil's soybean industry in the Mato Grosso region threatened by extreme weather events and shifting rainfall patterns driven by Amazon deforestation?'

A Literature and Performance extended essay must focus on both a written text (such as a novel or play) and a performance (such as a film, theatre staging or digital adaptation) of that piece.

Subject-specific knowledge questioning guide

Early in the process, as students are brainstorming topics or when they are designing research questions, it is helpful to have them assess their knowledge and understanding of their subject.

1 Create a concept map

In their RRS, have the student create a concept map with their subject at the centre.

2 Expand on key elements

Ask students to branch out with everything they know about:

- required sources/evidence types
- research methodologies
- subject-specific terminology
- common pitfalls.

While they work, note areas where the map is sparse or contains misconceptions.

3 Discuss and reflect

Review the map together, asking probing questions such as:

- What constitutes valid evidence in this subject?
- How will you approach analysis in this field?
- What subject-specific frameworks might you apply?

Encourage students to fill gaps in understanding by referencing the subject-specific guidance. Suggest faculty members who might provide additional subject expertise; identify specific readings or skills development needed.

Combining subjects in an interdisciplinary extended essay

Chapter 5 offers guidance on planning an interdisciplinary essay, but there is no single 'correct' way to integrate two subjects. In fact, there are many possible approaches that allow students to effectively demonstrate their understanding of each subject's unique methodologies and perspectives.

To begin, students might compile a list of the frameworks, concepts, approaches, and knowledge-making practices associated with each subject they are considering. Creating a Venn diagram can help visualise areas of overlap between the subjects, highlighting shared methodologies, theories, or areas of inquiry.

With this diagram in mind, students can reflect on their potential topic: Which elements from each subject are most relevant to their investigation? Are there natural points of connection that could guide a meaningful and coherent integration of the two disciplines?

Example

Sean enjoys reading and interpreting literature, but has been intrigued by activities in his Language A: literature class in which students were asked to quantify and track particular literary and poetic devices. He wondered how he might use what he has learned in Computer Science to complete that kind of work, which then led him to wonder about the limitations of both subjects in arriving at literary interpretation. He made a Venn diagram of the methods, theories and concepts of both courses, and noticed that the middle portion of the diagram showed how both disciplines look for patterns and then try to generate meaning from those patterns; both can use systematic observation to organise information, and both subjects rely to some extent on logic and reasoning to make valid interpretations of data. Where they differ is in their approach to ambiguity, since the sciences tend to eliminate ambiguity while literature often embraces it. The following diagram displays the key similarities and differences he identified as a result of his Venn diagram.

Literature	Shared concepts/goals	Computer Science
• focuses on human expressions, emotion, and artistic meaning • explores and interprets the human experience • often subjective and open to interpretation, ambiguity and multiple valid interpretations • qualitative	• deal with languages • require careful attention to syntax and formatting • involve understanding how smaller components build into large meaningful structures • require breaking down complex systems (texts/programs) into component parts • emphasise understanding context and purpose • involve studying patterns and their significance • require critical thinking about how different elements interact • combine theoretical understanding with practical application • require balancing creativity with technical constraints • consider how humans interact with and interpret the work • emphasise user/reader experience • require understanding human psychology and behaviour • deal with how meaning is constructed and interpreted	• solves concrete problems and creates functional systems • creates efficient, reliable solutions • outcomes are typically measurable and testable • values precision and unambiguous specifications • quantitative

Subjects: Computer Science and Literature

Research question: 'To what extent do Natural Language Processing algorithms interpret and analyse metaphors in contemporary poetry, such as that of Ocean Vuong, better than traditional literary analysis methods?'

For this extended essay, Sean wanted to see how something subjective like poetry might be analysed in a more objective, mathematical way. He decided to compare his understanding and analysis of Ocean Vuong's poetry to the pattern recognition, structural analysis, and algorithms of his Computer Science course. Doing so allowed him to reach the following insights:

- how algorithms might miss layers of meaning that human readers catch
- why certain types of metaphors are harder to detect computationally
- how machine learning could enhance (but not replace) literary analysis
- where human interpretation and computational analysis complement each other
- what computational analysis reveals about patterns in metaphor construction that humans might miss.

Reflection

Consider your own understanding of subject-specific requirements for the extended essay. This will help you identify areas where you may need additional support to guide your students. Ask yourself:

- What are the IB subject areas where I feel most confident providing guidance?
- Which subject areas might I need additional support with? (Consider reaching out to colleagues who teach these subjects.)
- For interdisciplinary essays, which subject combinations would I feel comfortable supervising?
- How might my own academic background influence how I approach different subjects?
- What resources do I need to better understand the requirements for subjects outside my expertise?

Commitment to success

The subject-specific nature of the extended essay reflects something profound about education itself: that knowledge is not uniform but varies in its methods, evidence, and expressions across different domains of human understanding. By helping students navigate these disciplinary waters, you are not just supporting an academic requirement – you are initiating them into the rich traditions of how we create and validate knowledge in diverse fields. As you guide students through the specific demands of their chosen subjects, you are helping them discover not just what they know, but how they know it. This metacognitive understanding represents one of the most valuable gifts the extended essay offers – a deeper awareness of how knowledge itself is constructed and validated.

Key takeaways: Chapter 6

- Students must understand the specific requirements and methodologies of their chosen subject(s) to create a successful extended essay.
- Each subject area has unique expectations regarding sources, research methodologies, subject-specific terminology and concepts, and analysis frameworks and approaches.
- Supervisors should direct students to review subject-specific guidance, even for subjects they are studying in their Diploma Programme.
- Interdisciplinary essays require careful consideration of how two subjects complement each other and clear justification for why both are necessary.
- While students bear ultimate responsibility for understanding requirements, supervisors can provide valuable guidance by connecting them with appropriate resources and faculty members.

Key term

artefact: a human-made object or creation that represents or reflects aspects of a culture, such as written documents, media productions (newspapers, magazines, films), artistic creations (works of fine art, architecture) and cultural expressions (fashion items, food dishes and brands) when analysed as manifestations of culture

7 Supervision strategies

This chapter covers the following:

- Effective supervision strategies
- Building a productive working relationship
- Progress monitoring tools and the Researcher's Reflection Space
- Intervention strategies
- Ensuring academic integrity

Effective supervision strategies

Although the extended essay is designed to be led by the students themselves, they still need careful supervision and intentional support. This is a learning experience for them, so anything you can do to help students identify and practise both academic and personal skills will increase their chances of success. And, as you saw in Chapter 1, student success means overall programme success!

Guided by input from supervisors, other faculty members and administration, extended essay coordinators should identify the most common challenges or skill gaps their students face, then design targeted lessons and assignments to tackle these issues. For example, coordinators might survey experienced extended essay supervisors and other faculty on the following areas.

Assessment

- In which criteria do students typically score lowest and why?
- Which aspects of the assessment criteria do students struggle to understand or to demonstrate?
- What are the most common reasons that extended essays do not reach the higher mark bands?
- In your experience, what distinguishes exceptional extended essays from average ones?

The extended essay process

- At what stage in the process do students most commonly fall behind or experience trouble?
- What school-established task or milestone have you found most effective for students?

Subject-specific considerations

- What unique challenges do students face when writing extended essays in your subject area?
- Which research methods in your subject prove most difficult for students?
- What types of research questions tend to be too ambitious or too narrow?
- What subject-specific resources do your students often overlook?
- What are the most common misunderstandings relating to academic conventions in your subject?

General challenges

- What writing issues do you consistently see across different student extended essays or other assignments in your subject?
- What misconceptions do students have about the research or writing process?

Support strategies

- What interventions have you found most effective for struggling students?
- How do you help students who are having difficulty finding appropriate sources?
- What strategies help students develop stronger analytical skills?
- How do you support students who struggle with time management or communication?

Preparation and training (supervisor and student)

- What preparation could students receive earlier in their academic careers that would better prepare them for the extended essay?
- What skills should be more thoroughly developed in IB coursework, before students begin the extended essay?
- What resources or training would help you better support extended essay students?
- How could collaboration between subject teachers improve extended essay outcomes?
- Regarding the extended essay, what do you wish you had more time to do?
- How has the extended essay process or student approach changed in recent years?
- What patterns have you noticed in successful versus unsuccessful extended essays?
- What one change do you feel would most improve student outcomes on the extended essay?

Once coordinators have gathered this data, they can confer with the IB coordinator and with administration to address the challenges that have been identified, and to insert scaffolding or explicit instruction into the extended essay process.

Remember

It is helpful to remind students that the skills and tasks required by the extended essay are, in general, the same as those they are developing and using in their IB Diploma Programme courses. The difference is that the extended essay needs to be a longer, more in-depth piece of writing.

Insights

'Participating in this focused discussion about the extended essay process has been incredibly valuable. After seven years of supervising extended essays across different subject areas, I've realised how much tacit knowledge we develop but rarely share with colleagues. The most significant insight for me was realising how much we could improve student outcomes by aligning our expectations and strategies across departments. When we speak with a unified voice about research methods and analytical frameworks – while still honouring disciplinary differences – we provide students with consistent guidance that builds their confidence throughout this challenging process'.

Beatrice P., IB Extended Essay Supervisor, History and Global Politics

Building a productive working relationship

Chapter 3 explored using informal check-in sessions and the required formal reflection sessions. Chapter 8 offers more detailed guidance for conducting the formal meetings. It is important to set expectations and boundaries early in your working relationship with the student. The extended essay is student-directed to develop communication and self-management skills, and to teach them to execute a long-term, larger project independently.

Setting expectations and boundaries

Your first meeting (whether informal or formal) is the ideal time to establish expectations and boundaries for the supervisor–student relationship. This will ensure students understand both your role and their responsibilities. Consider the following points for your initial meeting.

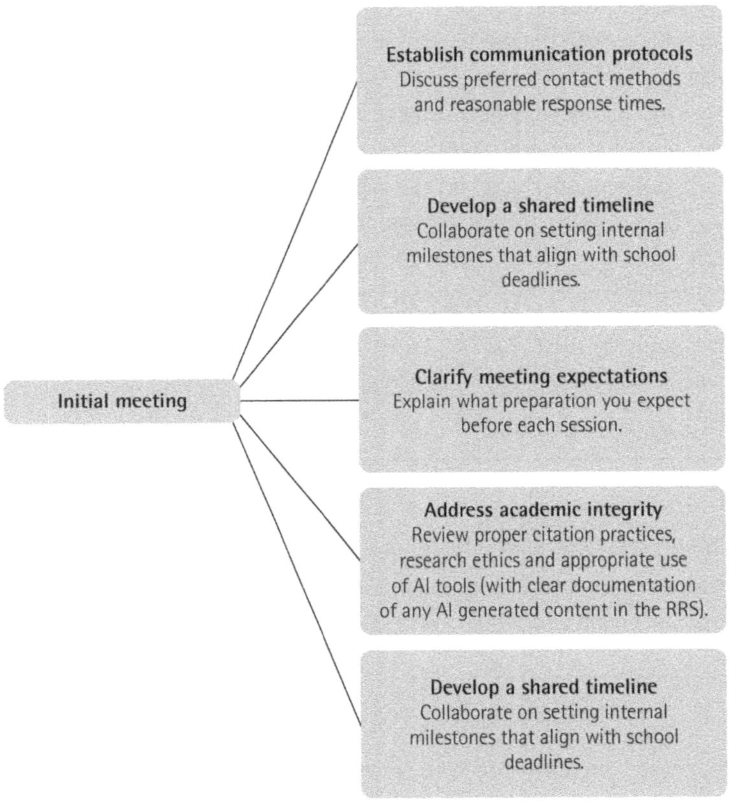

Defining your supervisory approach

Be explicit about what students can expect from you in terms of:

- the nature of feedback you provide (conceptual guidance versus detailed commentary)
- your areas of expertise and their limitations (see Chapter 5)
- your expectations for students regarding deadlines and meeting preparation
- Your school's and the IB's guidelines on appropriate use of AI tools (see Chapter 9).

Insights

'I've learned to create a simple "supervision agreement" that I discuss with students during our first meeting. This document outlines my expectations about meeting preparation, response times to emails, and the kind of feedback I'll provide. It also clarifies that while I'll guide them through the process, the research and writing remain their responsibility. This clear communication prevents misunderstandings later when deadlines approach'.

Maria E., Extended Essay Supervisor

Progress monitoring tools and the Researcher's Reflection Space

There are many options and a variety of tools available to schools to help track student progress, but these do not have to be sophisticated to be useful. The IB has established the Researcher's Reflection Space (RRS) as a tool for tracking students' progress, and highly recommends its use. The RRS is a space in which students keep all their records, notes, writing and reflections. Your school can decide what format the RRS takes – whether online (such as in Google Drive or a learning management software), or in physical notebooks or folders, or a combination of both. Tracking progress can then be as simple as checking the material in that RRS at regular intervals.

Recording AI use in the RRS

The RRS is a valuable space for students to document use of AI tools during the extended essay process. Encourage them to record interactions such as brainstorming, research support, or feedback on writing structure. While the IB requires transparency around AI use, these tools are not always cited in a traditional 'works cited' list, making the RRS an important place to capture this aspect of the student's work.

Students could include screenshots of AI prompts and responses, reflect on how the AI input shaped their thinking, or explain how they evaluated and incorporated AI-generated suggestions. This documentation helps supervisors **authenticate** work by providing an insight into the student's research and writing process, including when and how AI tools were utilised.

Remember

Supervisors should remind students that transparent documentation of authorised AI use demonstrates academic integrity rather than diminishing the originality of their work.

The Researcher's Reflection Space

The RRS serves many purposes.

For the student	For the supervisor
• It offers a dedicated workspace where students can develop a deeper, intentional connection with their project. • It helps keep them motivated as they can see the work they have already done. • It provides a dedicated area to note insights about readings, compositions and intellectual discoveries. • It helps students stay organised by keeping everything in one place. • It enhances readiness for feedback conversations with the supervisor. • It encourages students to record quick, informal reflections on what they are doing and on meetings with the supervisor. • It can serve as an archive of idea generation and questions for further exploration. • It can reveal how their perspective and reasoning evolved over the course of the process. • It becomes a valuable reference when crafting the reflective statement. • It acts as a portfolio of work to help ensure and demonstrate academic integrity. • It provides a template for practice in future projects once students see its benefits.	• It provides visibility into the student's thinking process and development. • It offers concrete evidence of student progress between supervision meetings. • It helps identify areas where students may need additional guidance or support. • It facilitates more productive and focused reflection sessions. • It allows supervisors to see how students are connecting with their chosen topic. • It reveals the depth of research and engagement with sources. • It shows the evolution of the student's line of argument. • It gives insight into the student's time management and planning. • It helps supervisors assess the authenticity of the student's work. • It provides a basis for meaningful feedback on the research process. • It assists in evaluating the student's reflection capabilities. • It creates opportunities for more personalised guidance based on documented progress.

Remember

The RRS is a wonderful tool to teach students the benefits of skills and habits, such as maintaining copies of sources and notes on those sources, reflecting regularly on what they are reading and thinking, and staying organised.

Whether the RRS is in digital or hard copy format, you could use some of the following ideas for its design and organisation.

1 **A single folder or file for each source (whether primary or secondary), which includes:**

- downloaded PDF copies of online sources such as scholarly articles
- data generated by surveys or experiments
- analysis and reflection notes on primary sources such as literary works, historical artefacts, visual or audio media, or raw data.

For research source material, remind students to:

- keep detailed bibliographic information on each source, including a **Digital Object Identifier (DOI)** for digital sources
- create and maintain a system (such as colour-coding) that helps them differentiate between exact quotes, paraphrased information, personal reactions or thoughts to source
- keep track of page numbers from which information or quotations are taken, as applicable.

2 **A folder or folders for reflections with dates recorded. The IB recommends that students write brief reflection notes after each required formal supervisor meeting (initial, interim and viva voce sessions) and throughout the process:**

- after informal meetings and check-ins
- after completing any internal tasks or deadlines that you give them, such as finalising their research question, creating a research plan, finding sources, writing an annotated bibliography, outlining, beginning to write, etc.

3 **A writing portfolio with copies of drafts and portions of drafts. This is a good way to demonstrate authentic work by keeping a paper trail of work done. Keeping drafts separate can also help students see the progress and changes they have made.**

4 **Records of any AI use. Instruct students to record specific prompts given to AI tools, their verbatim responses and a critical evaluation of these suggestions (what was accepted, rejected or modified and why). Include screenshots or copied text of exchanges with dates linked to corresponding research stages.**

As discussed in Chapter 3, additional meetings and check-ins are recommended to help keep students on track – and for students to update you on their progress.

Reflection

Take a moment to think about your own research and documentation practices, as well as how you might implement some of the suggestions and your own knowledge into your students' RRS use.

- How do your current supervision practices align with the strategies outlined in this chapter so far? What aspects might you want to strengthen or modify?
- Think about a successful extended essay you have supervised in the past. What specific supervision strategies contributed to that success? How might you replicate these with future students?
- Consider your communication style with students. Does it effectively balance providing guidance while promoting student independence? What adjustments might make your supervision more effective?
- How might you structure the Researcher's Reflection Space to best serve both your students' needs and your supervision requirements? What format (digital, physical or hybrid) would work best in your context?
- What specific guidance would you provide to help students effectively document their research process, including appropriate AI tool use?
- How could you use the RRS during supervision meetings to facilitate deeper student reflections and more meaningful progress conversations?

Intervention strategies

As educators, you will know that the learning process can be difficult, and often students run into challenges or lose motivation. You will also understand that there is no 'one size fits all' solution to student struggles. However, below are some suggestions for addressing various situations you might encounter as you support students through the extended essay process.

Procrastination or falling behind

- Use visual progress tracking tools such as **Kanban boards**. These systems help students see and gain satisfaction from tasks completed. They also help break down portions of a project into discrete tasks so progress feels achievable, and can help students identify where they get stuck, which – with supervisor support – can help them envision solutions.
- Assign smaller deliverables and reward their completion. Breaking down tasks such as an outline into smaller steps (for example, writing the thesis or outlining a body paragraph) will make the project feel more achievable and, if your school allows it, reward completion with a grade in a Diploma Programme course (such as theory of knowledge).
- Create peer accountability partners. Pair students to serve as accountability partners with structured check-in procedures.
- Arrange one-on-one conferences. The extended essay or IB coordinator or an administrator can hold a private discussion with a student to identify the root causes of avoidance (fear, being overwhelmed, lack of interest) rather than just the symptoms.

Research/writing challenges

- Set up targeted skill 'refresher' workshops. You might offer optional tutorials to address common challenges before the times they usually occur, such as how to conduct and write a literature review, how to analyse different types of data, or how to write in a formal, academic setting.
- Offer exemplars. Create opportunities for struggling students to read, discuss and assess sample extended essays in their subject. Provide them with annotated examples that highlight specific elements of strong extended essays.
- Model the task. Sometimes it can help to demonstrate the research or writing process in real-time (or on video that students can review later) in which the teacher thinks aloud and talks through the steps (and challenges) as they work.
- Allow alternate formats. Some students may benefit from using alternative formats on steps such as brainstorming (such as using mind maps or other visual portrayals), outlining (by creating graphics instead of written outlines to organise ideas) or writing (by using 'talk to text' tools to record and playback thinking).

Engagement issues

- Rekindle interest. Invite students to reflect on why they chose their topic, which element they were interested in, how their research might be connected to their life, or even have them share with someone else and invite questions and positive feedback from that person.

- Celebrate milestones and achievements. There are countless ways to celebrate student success and doing so can reenergise and motivate students. For example:
  - Have visible 'progress tracking charts' posted in a classroom where students can add stickers or symbols as tasks are completed.
  - Highlight students of the week.
  - Send students personalised notes or 'kudos'.
  - Create awards or tokens to hand out.
  - Set up small group discussions where students can share progress and encourage each other.
- Reduce the load temporarily. If students are really struggling, it can help to identify a smaller, achievable next step that can rebuild confidence.
- Cultivate a growth mindset and reframe the narrative. As with any process of learning, it is important to help students see setbacks as normal and productive steps toward growth.
- Offer opportunities for rest and recreation. Even educators can forget that breaks increase productivity and efficiency. Create times and spaces to practise mindfulness or relaxation techniques, explore what it means to be resilient, and reflect on successes and examples of perseverance.

Insights

'Sometimes I feel overwhelmed when trying to balance my extended essay with all my other classes, sports and extracurricular activities. A couple of days during the extended essay, though, my school carved out time for us to play games, practise yoga or just rest, and it really helped me see that they understand the stress we feel and that they care about us'.

Charlie M., IB Diploma Programme candidate

Ensuring academic integrity

There are three common causes for breaches of academic integrity during the extended essay.

1. Stress and procrastination. Often students make careless citation mistakes or choose to 'cut corners' because they are running out of time on a deadline. Building in support and careful planning of smaller tasks and deadlines can ensure that students are not trying to write 4,000 words in one evening.
2. Lack of understanding of proper citation practices or AI tool use. Students may make mistakes because they do not know how or when to cite. Regular reviews – such as workshops – of proper citation practices can help students recognise and address knowledge gaps. Similarly, students may feel confused by or anxious about the use of AI tools. Offering explicit instruction on proper use of AI and its benefits can help students understand how and why to use these tools ethically. Offering time for students to think about and discuss the reasons people may resort to unethical use can be helpful as well, as these discussions can offer a safe space to think more critically about ethics and what it means to be a principled student.
3. Lack of knowledge or confidence regarding steps of the process (such as reading scholarly work or writing analytical essays). As you have seen, teaching the required skills and competencies for success in the extended essay (and other IB Diploma Programme requirements) can build confidence, which keeps students engaged and willing.

Authenticating student work

All extended essays must be authenticated at the school site before they are sent to IB for marking. The IB's scaffolded process for the extended essay naturally supports authentication of student work. Through regular check-ins, reflection sessions and use of the RRS, supervisors develop familiarity with each student's writing style, thinking processes and capabilities. This process not only guides students but also enables supervisors to authenticate work with confidence.

When there appears to be a disconnect between the work produced and what has been observed during supervision, it is essential to have a thoughtful conversation with the student. Rather than relying solely on AI detection tools, which can produce false positives, focus on process-based authentication: ask students to explain their methodology, discuss their research journey, or elaborate on specific sections of their work. This approach maintains academic integrity while respecting students as developing scholars who are learning to navigate both traditional and emerging research tools.

Remember

Regular check-ins, the formal, required meetings and the RRS ensure students are not only staying on track but that they can demonstrate authentic, original work.

Commitment to success

Your belief in your students' capabilities, especially during moments of struggle, often becomes the catalyst for their breakthrough moments. When you provide thoughtful supervision, you are not just helping students complete an assignment, you are also cultivating lifelong skills in research, critical thinking and perseverance. Think of each check-in, each piece of feedback and each moment of encouragement as seeds you are planting; seeds that will continue to grow long after the extended essay is submitted.

Key takeaways: Chapter 7

- While the extended essay is student-directed, effective supervision requires intentional support and guidance.
- The Researcher's Reflection Space (RRS) is a highly recommended tool for tracking student progress and can be digital, physical – or a combination of both.
- The RRS benefits both students (by providing organisation, motivation and reflection space) and supervisors (by offering visibility into student progress and thinking).
- Recommended RRS organisation includes separate folders for sources, reflections, and writing drafts with proper documentation.
- Timely, focused intervention can help address student issues.
- Academic integrity issues often stem from stress/procrastination, lack of understanding about citation or AI use, and lack of confidence in the research process.
- Regular check-ins and maintaining the RRS help ensure students stay on track and can demonstrate authentic work.

Key terms

authenticate: to verify that the work submitted by students is genuinely their own

Digital Object Identifier (DOI): a unique alphanumeric code assigned to digital content that provides a permanent, reliable link to locate that content online (even if website content or address changes)

Kanban board: a visual project management tool that helps students visualise work, track progress and optimise efficiency

8 Reflection meetings and the reflective statement

This chapter covers the following:

- The importance of reflection throughout the extended essay process
- The three formal reflection sessions (initial, interim and viva voce)
- The reflective statement
- The reflection and progress form (RPF)

The importance of reflection throughout the extended essay process

Reflection is a core tenet of all IB programmes and, as such, has been built into the extended essay process. Students compose a 500-word reflective statement at the end of the process, following the viva voce. Practising and documenting reflection throughout will enable students to write a meaningful final reflection. However, the importance of reflection extends far beyond this piece of writing, as it develops students' metacognitive and self-management skills, which will serve them well in all aspects of their lives. Indeed, studies reveal the benefits of reflection and metacognition on people's professional success and personal well-being.

Metacognitive skills

By cultivating metacognitive skills in students, you will enhance their development across all aspects of life, while naturally complementing the spectrum of Approaches to Learning competencies (research, thinking, social, communication and self-management).

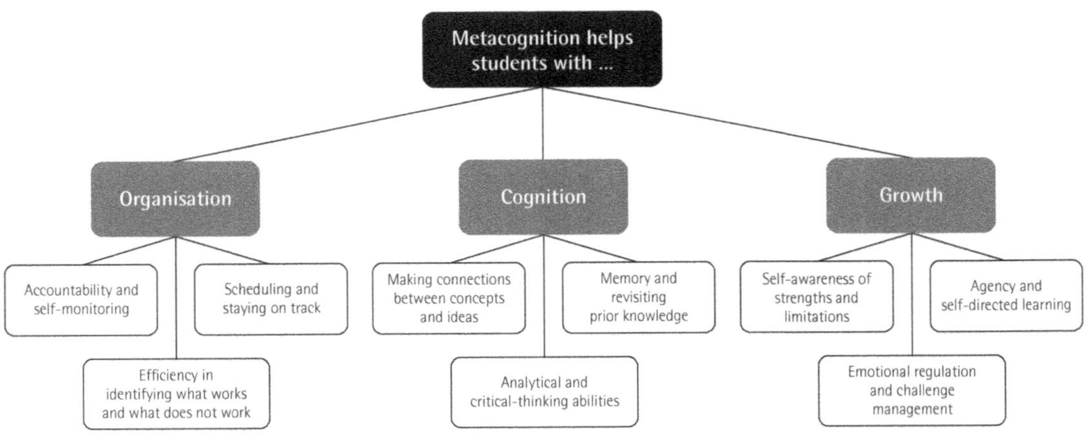

Remember

Nurturing metacognition in all the Approaches to Learning skills helps students with adaptability, resilience, independence and agency. These traits will help them in their Diploma Programme courses as well as in higher education, their career and their personal lives.

Cultivating a reflective mindset

Below are some ideas on how you could include opportunities for productive reflection in the extended essay process. Examples of templates for some of these activities can be found in the Appendix to this book.

'Start, stop, continue' activity

Start: List new behaviours or actions that should be introduced.

Stop: List current behaviours or actions that are not working and should be eliminated.

Continue: List current behaviours or actions that are working well and should be maintained.

This kind of reflection can be helpful throughout the process, but particularly in the initial and interim phases (see 'The three formal reflection sessions' below).

Small group reflection sessions

Schedule times for students to discuss progress, challenges and discoveries together. Giving them structured but open-ended questions to ask each other will teach them to take ownership of their thoughts and feelings, and to listen actively.

Goal-setting and self-assessment

At the beginning of each phase, have students identify two achievable goals for this phase. At the halfway and end point of the stage, assign an RRS reflection in which they assess themselves honestly and identify steps for improvement, if needed.

Relevance

During scheduled reflection times (and in their Diploma Programme courses), encourage students to make connections to their daily lives, to our global society, to what they are learning in another course, and so on. Helping them realise the applicability and significance of their research can increase engagement and encourage higher-order integrative thinking.

Non-traditional reflection activities

Students may come to see reflection as just another task they must complete, so break up regular reflections with more creative formats that can 'shake up' their thinking. For example, they might write a short sales pitch explaining and inspiring interest in their topic to an imagined stranger, or they might draw visual representations of their current mindset, their journey so far and their challenges and achievements. Or they could write a letter to their past or future self about the extended essay.

Remember

Reflection serves as a 'mental mirror', allowing students to actively examine their own thinking processes. By regularly pausing to consider what they have learned, how they have learned it, and what challenges they faced, students develop the self-awareness necessary to identify effective learning strategies and knowledge gaps. This metacognitive practice transforms passive students into strategic thinkers who can monitor, evaluate, and adjust their Approaches to Learning – ultimately creating more independent, adaptable and confident students who take ownership of their educational journey.

The three formal reflection sessions (initial, interim and viva voce)

A positive working relationship between you and the student is crucial for success. It is grounded in the three required formal meetings, and enhanced by as many less formal check-in sessions as the you and the student feel is helpful.

The three, 20–30 minute formal reflection sessions should occur at the beginning, middle and end of the process. Each meeting will be slightly different; the three tables below suggest some ways to think about them, as well as some questions to guide the discussions between you and the student.

Some schools conduct the first formal meeting once a topic has already been established, while others schedule it while students are still exploring topics. For this reason, the goals and guiding questions in the tables for the initial and interim meetings should be considered flexible, depending on your school. Guiding questions for all meetings are intended as examples rather than an exhaustive or prescriptive checklist.

Insights

'At my first meeting with my extended essay supervisor, I was feeling really nervous. Our extended essay coordinator had told us that we, the students, were in charge of directing the process and even the meetings, but I was a little unsure how to do this. My supervisor immediately put me at ease by just talking to me, asking me about myself and my interests, how I was feeling about the process, and so on. He really had a great attitude and seemed excited about this whole process for me, which helped me feel more positive about the whole thing.'

Maxime, IB Diploma Programme graduate

Initial meeting: Planning, preparation and inquiry

Goals	Guiding questions for the supervisor
For students: • Establish or deepen supervisor-student relationship. • Discuss and establish goals (academic and personal). • Discuss preliminary areas of interest. • Discuss early research findings and questions (from background research and topic exploration). • Clarify expectations and assessment criteria, if necessary. • Understand how to organise the approach to the extended essay. • Discuss the two extended essay pathways. • Discuss topics and research questions. • Refine the research question. • Discuss subject-specific considerations such as **methodology**. • Discuss planning and establish some self-imposed deadlines or a research plan. • Self-assess strengths and areas for growth (such as ATLs and learner profile traits). Supervisors should use this meeting to: • set expectations regarding when and how they would like to be contacted (and how far in advance, when scheduling meetings), etc. • remind students that the extended essay is student-directed and that it is their responsibility to know and understand their subject(s), seek subject-specific guidance or help as needed, either from you or from a subject teacher or expert • confirm that students are aware of their responsibilities and of the scope and requirements of the extended essay • review what they are permitted to do and not permitted to do (such as edit writing).	• What has drawn you to this research topic, and what preliminary knowledge do you already have about it? • What do you know already about studies in this subject or subjects and what do you need to learn more about (for example, methods and methodology)? • Have you formulated a working research question that aligns with your subject's criteria and promotes analytical thinking? • How familiar are you with the extended essay requirements for your chosen subject area, and have you reviewed the relevant sections of the extended essay guidance? • Which pathway will you choose, and can you articulate why this pathway is the best choice for your topic? • What key sources have you identified so far, and what is your strategy for finding additional reliable resources? • What theoretical frameworks or methodologies are you planning to use, and are you aware of any ethical considerations related to your research? • Have you read and do you understand the assessment criteria? • What challenges have you encountered in your research process, and what steps are you taking to address them? • How are you organising your RRS, and what types of materials are you including to document your thinking process? • What timeline have you established for research, writing and revision, and how will you manage your time effectively? • What specific goals do you have between now and our next meeting? • How are you ensuring that your research approach is analytical rather than merely descriptive? • What steps are you taking to maintain balance during this process?

Interim meeting: Progress review and refinement

Goals	Guiding questions
For students: • Ask questions and discuss research findings, sources and initial analyses. • Consider methodology and structure for the essay. • Discuss early pieces of writing (such as the outline, annotated bibliography) and/or the draft of essay. Supervisors should use this meeting to: • ensure students have read and understand all guidance on writing the essay, on citing and documenting sources, and the assessment criteria • confirm that students are using sources and any tools such as AI-assisted research ethically and can speak confidently and independently about their work • remind students to maintain their schedule (which should include breaks and other forms of staying balanced and caring for their well-being) • direct students to extra help such as librarians or subject-area experts, if necessary.	• What progress have you made in your research so far, and how have you managed your approach? • What obstacles have you encountered, and how have you overcome them? (These might be academic challenges or they might relate to self-management skills.) • How are you maintaining your academic integrity and ensuring your work remains your own? • Has your research question evolved, and how has your understanding of the topic deepened or changed? • What adjustments to your research plan are necessary to successfully complete your essay? • How well are you satisfying the assessment criteria? • How coherent is your argument structure, and does it provide clear logical progression throughout? • Have you included sufficient evidence to support your claims, and have you critically evaluated this evidence? • What inconsistencies or weaknesses have you identified in your analysis that need addressing? • Are you spending more time analysing, discussing and evaluating than simply summarising, describing or reporting? • Will a reader be able to easily follow your reasoning from introduction to conclusion? • What are you learning about the subject(s), research, your topic, writing, and so on? • What connections can you make between your extended essay and your other coursework or the real world?

Final meeting (viva voce): Reflect and celebrate

<table>
<tr><th>Goals</th><th>Guiding questions</th></tr>
<tr><td>For students:
• Reflect on the entire research process.
• Discuss the final product.
• Consider what was learned about the topic and research process.
• Evaluate strengths and areas for improvement.
• Identify transferable skills that have been developed.

Supervisors should use this meeting to:
• remind students to take a moment and celebrate their success upon completion of the essay
• discuss the reflective statement and its assessment
• help students think through material to be included in the reflective statement
• ensure the authenticity of students' final work.</td><td>• To what extent has your thinking about your subject, topic and research question changed and why do you think this is so?
• What do you feel most proud of and why?
• If you were to repeat this process, what would you do differently, and why?
• What have you learned about yourself as a result of this process?
• What were some transformative moments for you (positive, negative or both)?
• How has this process prepared you for future study or work?
• What abilities, knowledge or skills might you take from this and how might you use them in the future?</td></tr>
</table>

Post-meeting reflections

At each meeting, remind students to record detailed notes of your discussion in their RRS. It is also a good idea to ask students to write a reflection, even an informal one, after the meeting.

These notes and reflections:

- help students remember and process what was discussed
- help track progress
- serve as evidence of the student's authentic work-in-progress
- provide concrete material and examples for the final reflection
- develop metacognitive skills (which build resilience, self-awareness and motivation).

The reflective statement

At the end of the process, after the viva voce, students compose a 500-word reflective statement. This will be entered on the reflection and progress form (RPF) and is assessed by Criterion E on a scale of 1–4 marks.

The reflective statement is a piece of writing that allows students to demonstrate their growth throughout the process and their ability to think critically about their own learning. Additionally, it offers a space for them to articulate how they will use their new knowledge and skills in future academic endeavours.

While there is no prescribed written structure for the reflective statement, it might include:

- new insights that emerged during the viva voce
- a discussion of skills gained (such as research methods, critical analysis, academic writing) and how they evolved over the process
- new or deeper knowledge acquired or connections made as a result of the research
- new perspectives gained or old assumptions challenged
- evaluation of effectiveness of habits, choices, methods, etc. used
- learner profile traits or Approaches to Learning, skills developed
- how this process has equipped them for future study or work
- how new skills might be applied to future contexts.

It is also important to include concrete examples in the reflective statement that illustrate the above.

It may be helpful to share some of the following 'dos and don'ts' with students.

Do ...	Don't ...
✓ be honest about challenges and mistakes – reflection includes acknowledging difficulties	✗ merely describe or list what you did
✓ balance discussion of strengths and weaknesses	✗ suggest lack of genuine engagement with the process or your topic
✓ use specific examples rather than generalisations	✗ remain superficial and general in your reflection
✓ think of both what you have learned and how you have changed	✗ focus only on what went well and ignore challenges
✓ keep the tone personal and authentic	✗ be too descriptive rather than truly reflective
✓ connect reflection to personal growth or future applications	✗ simply summarise the essay content instead of reflecting on the process
✓ explain how you have grown and changed as a result of the process	✗ make vague statements without specific examples
✓ include a few examples or evidence of that change – for example, a new understanding you experienced or an obstacle you overcame	✗ treat the reflective statement as merely an afterthought.
✓ identify how you might transfer your new knowledge and skills to other tasks or areas of life	
✓ evaluate how your thinking evolved or changed over the process	
✓ focus on the *how, why* and *so what* of the process	
✓ think of this final reflection as the culmination of your achievement and a time to step back and see how much you have learned and developed.	

Maximising success on Criterion E

As with the assessment of the essay itself, examiners will apply a 'best fit' approach to Criterion E and will reward what the student does well. There are two strands to this criterion: evaluative reflection and growth, and transfer of learning. Examiners want to see that students can both synthesise (their experiences and learning) and evaluate (their growth and development). Chapter 4 includes some ideas for how to guide students in both strands; here some general ideas to support students to write their reflective statements:

- Remind students of the importance of keeping detailed notes of reflections throughout the process.
- Ask open-ended questions during meetings, to help students own the process.
- 'Reflect back' when you witness a student articulate evidence of self-evaluation, realisation of growth or development, and so on. It may not always be obvious to a student that they are demonstrating growth or practising productive reflection, so calling attention to those times can help them recognise them in the future.
- Read and discuss written student reflections throughout the process. As students compose informal reflections and notes, make sure these not only describe but that they also self-analyse and self-evaluate. Encourage students to jot down specific moments or realisations so that they can reference them later as evidence.

High-scoring reflective statements reveal a student who is self-aware, can critically self-assess, and has engaged honestly and intentionally with the process to grow and develop as a person.

The Programme Resource Centre on the IB website has examples of marked reflective statements.

Reflection

Although the information here focuses on reflection for student success in the extended essay, you may also wish to apply the insights here to other subjects. Courses across the IB continuum involve intentional reflection, whether explicit or implicit. Think of the courses or material you teach or about your administrative practices:

- How am I helping students develop their international-mindedness and global perspectives?
- In what ways do I create opportunities for students to engage with the IB learner profile attributes in authentic contexts?
- Am I providing students with sufficient opportunities to develop their Approaches to Learning skills (thinking, communication, social, self-management, and research)?
- In what ways do I encourage student agency and voice in their learning journey?
- How am I supporting students in making meaningful connections between subjects and to life outside school?
- In what ways am I modelling lifelong learning and inquiry for my students?

The reflection and progress form (RPF)

The reflection and progress form is provided by the IB and can be found in the Programme Resource Centre. It serves several purposes:

- It records students' attendance at the three mandatory reflection sessions (three different dates).
- It is where students enter their reflective statement.
- Completion of this form attests to the authenticity of students' work.

It is important to remember that the RPF is a required component of the extended essay process: 'The completion of this form is a mandatory requirement of the extended essay. It must be submitted together with the completed essay [...]. Students and supervisors should be aware that a mark of 0 will be awarded by the examiner for criterion E if the RPF is blank or the reflective statement is written in a language other than that of the accompanying essay (International Baccalaureate 2023)'.

Commitment to success

While the extended essay is student-directed, you play a vital role in setting and maintaining a positive tone for the process. Often, your attitude – especially at the beginning of the process, when students can feel particularly overwhelmed or daunted by the project – can make a huge difference in their experience. Many times, students just need to be reminded of their own capabilities and encouraged to take risks and do their best. Help them remember that the extended essay is not just a task to be completed, but a journey of growth and self-discovery. Having said this, it is essential that you create an environment where students can express their frustrations and fears, and establish healthy boundaries. If you find that delicate balance between holding students accountable and providing encouragement, your students will flourish!

Key takeaways: Chapter 8

- Reflection is a core component of the extended essay process, developing students' metacognitive skills and self-management abilities that transfer to other aspects of their lives.
- Three formal reflection meetings (initial, interim and viva voce) are required throughout the process. Supervisors should set a positive, productive, intentional tone during these meetings, which will ripple out into the whole process.
- The initial reflection meeting focuses on establishing the supervisor-student relationship, discussing preliminary interests and questions, clarifying expectations, and developing a research plan. In the interim meeting, the student reviews progress, discusses challenges and solutions, and plans next steps while the supervisor provides feedback on the work thus far. The viva voce (final meeting) reflects on the entire process and prepares students for writing their reflective statement.
- The 500-word reflective statement is completed after the viva voce and assessed under Criterion E (worth 1–4 marks). It should demonstrate students' growth throughout the process, include specific examples, and articulate how they will apply their new knowledge and skills in future academic endeavours.
- Assessment of the reflective statement focuses on two strands: Evaluation (how well students assess themselves as students with specific examples) and Growth (evidence of development throughout the process and identification of transferable skills).
- Documenting reflection throughout the process is crucial – students should maintain detailed notes in their Researcher's Reflection Space (RRS) after each meeting. These notes help track progress, serve as evidence of authentic work, provide material for the final reflection and develop metacognitive skills.

Key term

methodology: a broad theoretical framework and approach that justifies why certain research methods were selected and how they align with the research question

9 Research skills and support

This chapter covers the following:

- Research skills development
- The importance of librarians
- Supporting students with AI tools in research

Research skills development

The extended essay develops and strengthens three important elements of research skills: a spirit of inquiry, critical-thinking skills, and academic integrity.

A spirit of inquiry

To build lifelong students, it is important to cultivate a sense of wonder, a willingness to take risks and a desire to broaden one's perspectives. The extended essay gives students agency over subject(s) and topics they write about; it is ideal for fulfilling these aims. Asking open-ended questions of your students during your meetings with them is one way to model inquiry. Asking follow-up questions to each response can show students how knowledge comes in those moments that require deeper thought about assumptions and existing knowledge. An example of such a conversation is shown below.

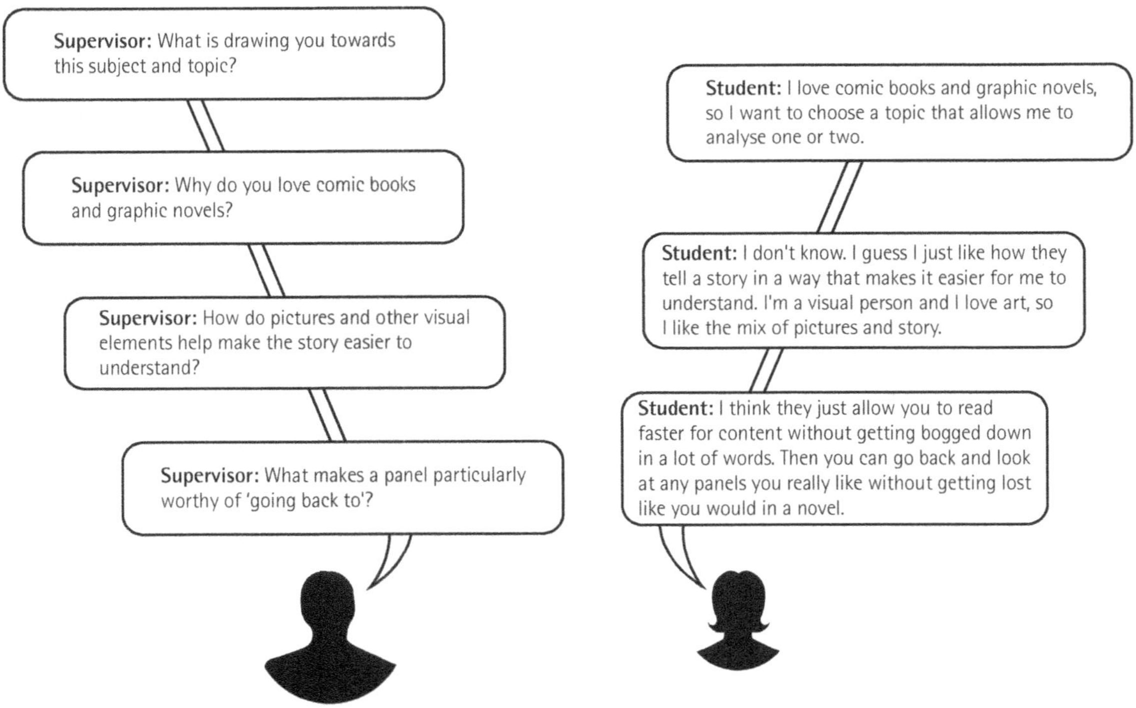

This conversation encourages the student to pause and critically reflect on a primary source – such as a graphic novel – and consider what makes it unique as a literary form. From there, the discussion might explore specific styles, themes, or how images affect the reader (especially if the student is pursuing the interdisciplinary pathway, such as combining Literature and IB Psychology).

The goal of these sessions is not to reach a fixed conclusion but to give the student space to think out loud and reflect intentionally. This process can build confidence in their subject understanding or open new directions for inquiry.

Critical-thinking skills

Students are bombarded with information and media daily, so it is important that they know how to engage with material critically, and to evaluate its construction, purpose, effectiveness and impact. Students must become thinking consumers of media; researching their extended essays provides a space to practise this skill. Here are some examples of how coordinators and supervisors can help students develop their information literacy.

Coordinators

Coordinators can create interim assignments, such as source reviews or annotated bibliographies, to ensure that students are carefully reading and analysing their primary and secondary sources. In these cases, mnemonics such as SMART (**S**ource, **M**otivation, **A**ccuracy, **R**elevance and **T**imeliness) or SIFT (**S**top, **I**nvestigate, **F**ind better, **T**race claims) are helpful. Explicit instruction and modelling of source evaluation is also helpful. (The importance of librarians and media specialists in teaching these skills is discussed later in this chapter.)

Supervisors

Supervisors can discuss sources and source evaluation with students during check-in meetings as well as in formal reflection meetings, using questions such as:

- In what ways have you challenged or verified the information presented in this source?
- How does this source compare with others you have found in terms of perspective, methodology or conclusions?
- Are there any significant disagreements between this source and others? How do you account for these differences?
- What patterns or consensus do you notice when examining multiple sources on your topic?
- How has your understanding of the topic evolved as you have engaged with multiple sources?
- Which sources have been most influential in shaping your thinking, and why?
- How will you incorporate this source's information, ideas or perspectives into your essay?
- What specific quotes, data or concepts from this source are most valuable for supporting your argument?
- How might you acknowledge the limitations of this source while still using it effectively?
- How does this source help you address potential counterarguments to your thesis?
- In what ways has this source influenced your thinking about your research question or thesis statement?

These questions are also good ones to give students if they will be writing annotated bibliographies.

Academic integrity

Obviously, you need to ensure that students do their own writing, but it is also important that they understand proper academic citation: what it is, how to do it and why it matters. Often, students commit academic misconduct not because they are trying to deliberately deceive, but because they have insufficient understanding of citation. Make sure students have access to and understand the IB's academic honesty guidance.

Below are some ideas for teaching (or reinforcing) proper citation:

- **Citation scavenger hunt:** Have students analyse exemplary extended essays to identify different types of citations and discuss their purpose.
- **Annotated bibliography practice:** Assign mini annotated bibliographies before the full extended essay to build the habit of evaluating sources.
- **Citation style workshops:** Create hands-on sessions focusing on the specific citation style relevant to their subject area.
- **Peer review sessions:** Have students check each other's citations and provide feedback.
- **Researcher's Reflection Space:** Remind students to make use of their RRS to document sources as they find them, rather than trying to relocate them later.
- **'Cite as you write':** Teach students to cite as they go along.

Remember

Many students fall into the trap of thinking they will add citations later, but this is a bad idea. Remind them that because the extended essay takes months to complete, they may:

- forget where they found specific information
- not recall which words were theirs and which came directly from a source
- misidentify which ideas came from which sources.

The IB considers all these mistakes academic misconduct, whether they commit them by accident or on purpose. Being forgetful or disorganised is no excuse! So, remind them to use their RRS. Every time they take notes from a source, they should:

- indicate direct quotations with quotation marks; even if they end up paraphrasing the quotation later, doing so will help them remember whose words were whose
- write down complete source information
- note page numbers for quotations and key ideas
- add their own thoughts separately.

Reflection

Take a moment to think about your own teaching practice, and how the information in this chapter so far relates to your course. How might supervising an extended essay allow you to strengthen your own pedagogical practices based on the essay's aims? Consider the following:

- How effectively am I implementing open-ended questioning techniques to cultivate a spirit of inquiry in my students?
- In what ways am I modelling critical thinking rather than just teaching or advising on content?
- How well do I balance giving students direction versus allowing them space to develop their own thinking?
- How effectively am I addressing academic integrity in a way that teaches proper citation rather than just warning against plagiarism?
- Am I creating opportunities for students to 'think out loud' and examine their assumptions?
- In what ways do I help students recognise patterns or conflicts across multiple sources?
- In what ways am I helping students connect their personal interests to their academic studies?

The importance of librarians

The importance of librarians to student success in the extended essay cannot be overstated. In the IB context, the library is more than just a resource centre – it is the intellectual hub of the school, a vital node in the learning community that supports inquiry across disciplines. Librarians are trained information specialists who not only know how to navigate academic databases, maximise search strategies and evaluate sources, but also understand how to guide students toward credible, relevant and often hard-to-find materials.

With years of expertise, librarians help students move beyond random searching to conduct systematic, purposeful literature reviews and to manage their research notes and citations effectively. More than that, librarians model the IB learner profile in action: they are the ultimate inquirers, thinkers and communicators. Their role is deeply synergistic, working in close collaboration with extended essay supervisors and coordinators to help students develop the research, critical thinking and academic integrity skills that are essential for success – not only in the extended essay, but at university and beyond.

Below are some ways that extended essay coordinators can harness the expertise of their school librarians throughout the extended essay process.

Developing information literacy

Throughout the **IB continuum**, librarians can help students learn how to:

- devise effective search strategies
- evaluate source credibility and relevance
- understand academic citation systems
- distinguish between primary and secondary sources
- navigate copyright and academic integrity issues.

If students have not had adequate training or experience before they enter the Diploma Programme, they may benefit from explicit instruction by librarians on all the above skills.

Offering guidance through the extended research process

The extended essay is often a student's first sustained experience with independent academic research. It challenges students to take ownership of their inquiry, navigate complexity and reflect meaningfully on both process and product. In this journey, the librarian is not just a resource expert – they are a critical partner in nurturing research confidence and academic curiosity.

Because of their expertise in research methodologies, academic integrity and information literacy, librarians are well positioned to collaborate with extended essay coordinators in shaping a thoughtful, developmentally appropriate extended essay process. Their insights can support the planning and pacing of internal deadlines, the scaffolding of research skills, and the design of learning experiences that align with the IB's emphasis on independent inquiry.

Librarians support the extended essay process by:

- creating logical research checkpoints aligned with library and digital literacy development
- offering insight into realistic timelines for different phases of the research cycle
- designing targeted workshops that address common research challenges
- advising on relevant database subscriptions and resource acquisitions
- curating subject-specific research pathways and collections tailored to IB subject groups.

Providing access to subject-specific resources

IB librarians typically maintain curated collections of academic journals, databases and reference materials that align with the needs of different subject areas. By helping students access credible, subject-specific resources, librarians support deeper, more scholarly engagement with the research topic. This is an essential step in moving from surface-level investigation to sustained academic inquiry.

Offering technological support

Independent research requires digital fluency. Librarians play a key role in helping students:

- use citation management tools to organise sources
- access academic databases remotely and ethically
- evaluate digital content with a critical, reflective lens
- manage digital research materials with academic discipline.

Supporting well-being

The extended essay is intellectually demanding and often emotionally challenging. Librarians create a supportive research environment that encourages resilience and reflection by:

- offering encouragement and a non-evaluative listening ear when students hit obstacles in their research path
- providing guidance or feedback beyond what the subject supervisor may be able to offer
- maintaining quiet, focused research spaces that promote balance and productivity
- normalising the iterative, non-linear nature of research and inquiry.

Supporting supervisors

Librarians also support supervisors by:

- briefing them on specialised research tools and subject-specific resources
- offering clarification on evolving issues like research ethics and the use of generative AI
- creating ready-to-use resource guides and support materials tailored to supervisor needs.

Remember

The extended essay is more than a research paper; it is an intellectual rite of passage for IB students. By modelling the learner profile traits – especially being inquirers, thinkers and reflective practitioners – librarians guide students in bridging the gap between school and university-level research. When schools involve their media specialists from the beginning of the extended essay process through to completion, they strengthen the entire learning community and deepen the inquiry experience for everyone involved.

Insights

'Supporting the extended essay process is one of the best parts of my job – after all, research is what I love! I really enjoy supporting not just the students but my colleagues as well. I want to encourage other schools to call on their librarians, as we are ready and waiting to help!'

Zhang L., school librarian

Supporting students with AI tools in research

It is important that supervisors help students understand how to use AI tools ethically and responsibly, while maintaining academic integrity. The IB recognises that AI technologies are increasingly part of academic work and does not prohibit their use. However, it does emphasise that students should employ these tools purposefully and transparently.

When discussing AI use with students, emphasise the following key principles:

- AI should function as a tool that *supports* learning, rather than replacing student thinking and work.
- The extended essay must remain fundamentally the student's own intellectual work.

- Students must be transparent about their use of AI tools, particularly during reflection sessions.
- Students should understand both the capabilities and limitations of AI tools.

Appropriate uses of AI in research

Guide students to understand how AI can be appropriately used in their extended essay process.

Topic exploration and brainstorming

AI can help generate initial ideas, suggest connections between concepts, or identify dimensions of a topic students might not have considered.

Resource discovery

AI-enhanced research tools can visualise connections between scholarly works and identify research pathways that students might not discover through conventional searches (although traditional academic databases remain essential).

Understanding complex ideas

AI can summarise difficult concepts to help students grasp foundational knowledge before developing their own analysis.

Organisation and planning

AI can help students organise research materials and develop research timelines.

Limitations of AI to discuss with students

Students should be aware of critical limitations when using AI tools.

AI complements but does not replace subject expertise

While AI can access and synthesise vast amounts of information, it lacks the depth of understanding and critical judgement that comes from years of specialised study and practice in a field. This is precisely why your role as supervisor is invaluable – you bring authentic expertise and can help students distinguish between surface-level information and deeper conceptual understanding. Your guidance helps students develop their own analytical skills to evaluate the relevance and accuracy of AI-generated content.

AI responds to inputs rather than understanding nuance

The quality of AI outputs depends heavily on the quality of inputs provided. At present, AI tools cannot truly grasp the subtle contextual factors, conceptual nuances or theoretical frameworks that inform scholarly research. As a supervisor, you provide that crucial human dimension – helping students detect significance, navigate ambiguity and make intuitive connections across disparate ideas. Your conversations with students about their research will help them develop these uniquely human strengths that AI cannot replicate.

AI can 'hallucinate'

A **hallucination** is when AI presents incorrect information confidently or creates false citations. Your expertise as a supervisor is essential in helping students verify facts, quotations and references from reliable academic sources and in teaching them to approach AI-generated information with appropriate scepticism.

Prohibited uses of AI

These uses of AI should be explicitly identified as violations of academic integrity:

- Having AI write paragraphs, sections or entire drafts of the essay.
- Using AI-generated research questions without significant modification and personal input.
- Asking AI to create reflections for the RPF.
- Using AI to translate an essay from one language to another for submission.
- Attempting to hide AI use.

Guiding students on transparency with AI use

When students use AI tools in their research process, advise them to maintain a record in their RRS of which AI tools they used, what prompts they used, and how they incorporated or verified the information.

Discuss their AI use during reflection sessions; this provides an opportunity to:

- evaluate the relevance and accuracy of AI-generated insights
- consider how the AI tool helped deepen their understanding
- reflect on their own thinking process in relation to the AI assistance.

Include a brief note in their methodology section explaining how AI tools assisted their research process. For example: 'As part of my research methodology, I utilised ChatGPT to help organise my initial literature search and identify potential connections between theories. All factual information and academic analysis presented in this essay are supported by proper scholarly sources as cited.'

School policies and regulations

Remind students to seek out and follow school-specific guidelines about AI use before incorporating these tools. As a supervisor, you should:

- be familiar with your school's policies on AI use in academic work
- understand any regional or national regulations that might apply
- consider equity issues, as not all students have equal access to these tools
- consult with the extended essay coordinator about any questions regarding AI use.

Supporting reflective practice with AI

Encourage students to reflect on how AI tools may have influenced their thinking. Help them distinguish between their own intellectual contributions and AI assistance, and guide them to consider how AI might be used ethically in future academic work. Use the reflection sessions to assess how well students understand the appropriate boundaries of AI use.

By discussing these guidelines with students early in the extended essay process, you can help them develop a thoughtful, ethical approach to incorporating AI tools in their research while maintaining academic integrity and developing their own scholarly skills.

Example

The following sample framework guides students in critically evaluating information generated by AI tools. It encourages them to assess AI outputs as they would any other source – by reading critically and questioning reliability. The framework reinforces that AI should be a starting point for inquiry, not an authority, and that students remain responsible for verifying, evaluating, and contextualising all information.

Assess accuracy:

- Can I find this same information in at least two credible academic sources?
- Does the AI provide specific citations that I can locate and verify?
- Are there any claims that seem implausible or contradict established knowledge in the field?

Source transparency:

- Can I trace the lineage of this information to its original academic source?
- Is this information potentially outdated given the AI's training cutoff date?
- How might my phrasing of the prompt have influenced the response?

Detect bias:

- Does the information present multiple viewpoints or just dominant perspectives?
- Are there cultural assumptions embedded in this information?
- How might systematic biases in training data affect this response?

Depth analysis:

- Does this response go beyond surface-level information?
- Does the response acknowledge complexity and nuance in the topic?
- Are methodological considerations or limitations addressed?

Context relevance:

- How well does this information apply to my specific research context?
- Does this information reflect current thinking in the field?
- Is this information relevant to the specific scope of my extended essay?

Commitment to success

As you help students develop their spirit of inquiry, critical thinking and academic integrity, remember that you are not just supporting an assignment – you are cultivating skills that will serve them for a lifetime. By partnering with librarians, asking thoughtful questions and providing targeted feedback, you transform the extended essay from an intimidating task into a meaningful opportunity for growth. The time you invest in guiding students through this process empowers them to find their academic voice and experience the genuine satisfaction of scholarly achievement. Your mentorship today shapes the researchers, thinkers and writers of tomorrow.

Key takeaways: Chapter 9

- The extended essay helps develop three important research skills: a spirit of inquiry, critical thinking skills and academic integrity.
- Librarians play a crucial role in the extended essay process by developing students' information literacy, guiding research, providing subject-specific resources, offering technological support and supporting student wel -being.
- Supervisors can guide students towards ethical and thoughtful use of AI, helping them build critical digital literacy skills for university and beyond.
- Teaching proper citation and academic integrity is essential to prevent misconduct that often stems from students' incomplete understanding of citation practices.

Key terms

hallucination: AI-generated content that is factually incorrect, nonsensical, or not grounded in its training data or the information provided

IB continuum: the range of IB programmes for students from 3–19, which includes the Primary Years (PYP), Middle Years (MYP), Career Programme (CP) and the Diploma Programme (DP)

10 Guiding and reviewing student writing

This chapter covers the following:

- The structure of the extended essay
- The importance of analysis, evaluation and discussion
- Structure and formatting
- Academic writing guidance
- Reviewing the rough draft
- Citing, referencing and ethical research

The structure of the extended essay

There are two important aspects to consider when it comes to the structure of the extended essay: the formal IB requirements that govern how the essay should be presented and formatted, and the academic structure of the essay – how to organise ideas, arguments and evidence to effectively communicate the research. Both are essential for students' success.

Whether a student has chosen the single-subject or the interdisciplinary pathway, their essay should follow the general academic structure outlined on the following pages:

- Introduction
- Body
- Conclusion

The key components of each of these sections are shown below, along with an explanation of how they are evaluated by the assessment criteria. This information can help you as you review their rough draft, to ensure students are meeting all requirements.

Introduction

For some essays, one or two paragraphs will be enough to introduce the research question and note the context, worthiness and thesis. However, it is fine if the student needs several paragraphs for their introduction.

Below is an example of a structure for an introductory section to an extended essay that requires more than one paragraph. In fact, the term 'introduction' here is fluid because, depending on the student's subject(s), their methods and methodology might be more detailed and thus require their own section following the introduction. For example, an extended essay in the sciences will probably involve more detail on the design and execution of the experiment. This includes aspects such as variable control, replication protocols, statistical analysis methods, and equipment specifications. It may also contain a more extensive literature review that examines previous related studies, theoretical frameworks, and established methodologies. In contrast, a Literature essay would likely have a different focus.

Content	Assessment criteria
• Research question • **Research methods** • Methodology • Thesis statement and signposting of the essay's structure • Relevant background and context (this information should be brief, just a few sentences will do) • Clear justification of the worthiness and originality of the research question and, for an interdisciplinary pathway, of the choice of an interdisciplinary approach and selected subjects • Brief 'literature review' of the existing research and scholarship on their topic (which makes clear that the student understands their essay is part of a larger scholarly conversation)	• A: Framework for the essay (the research question and methods provide an effective framework for the essay). • B: Knowledge and understanding (of relevant and appropriate concepts, terminology and existing scholarship in the subject or subjects). • C: Analysis and line of argument (the thesis will begin to signpost their line of argument and its analysis).

Body

Most of the essay will be the body paragraphs. This is where the student builds a focused, reasoned argument based on their investigation and their analysis of the information, data and evidence. Depending on their selected subject(s), the structure and format of body paragraphs may vary, but the following guidelines apply to all essays. If the introduction does not mention methods, methodology, background/context (briefly), or a review of current scholarly literature, they should be included in the early body paragraphs.

Content	Assessment criteria
Distinct paragraphs, each of which features: • a topic sentence with a single focus • presentation of findings, data and observations • analysis and evaluation of data or source material • clear relevance to your line of argument • a balanced combination of claims, evidence and analysis/ discussion of how the evidence supports the claim. Body paragraphs should: • build upon each other • remain focused on the essay's line of argument • transition clearly and logically, using either transition/signal words or connections between ideas. Body paragraphs may be grouped using chapter headings or subheadings, as appropriate. Many body paragraphs will integrate the work of other scholars to support the argument, provide counterclaims, offer space for new ideas, and so on. Body paragraphs that evaluate methods and materials may occur at the end of the discussion and offer suggestions for future studies.	• A: Framework for the essay (the essay should follow the appropriate structure for the subject(s) chosen). • B: Knowledge and understanding (of relevant and appropriate concepts, terminology, existing scholarship in your subject(s)). • C: Analysis and line of argument (this section of the essay should consist primarily of their own thoughts, interpretations and analyses). • D: Discussion and evaluation (explain the significance of their findings and support their claims with appropriate and convincing evidence; offer a range of perspectives; evaluate their research methods, materials and findings – their strengths and limitations).

Conclusion

The conclusion to the extended essay may be more than one paragraph, depending on the subject and topic.

Content	Assessment criteria
• A return to the research question • Synthesis/review/summary of the discussion • Completion of the line of argument by connection to broader context/implications, showing relevance beyond the specific topic	• A: Framework (structure – including a thoughtful, meaningful conclusion). • B: Knowledge and understanding (demonstrate a careful analysis of research to develop a deep understanding of the topic). • C: Line of argument (the conclusion should feel like the natural endpoint of this line).

The importance of analysis, evaluation and discussion

The extended essay assessment criteria distinguish between analysis (Criterion C) and evaluation and discussion (Criterion D). While Chapter 4 introduced these distinctions in the context of assessment, this chapter explores how to help students apply these concepts in their writing. When reviewing students' drafts, look for evidence of all three elements to ensure they are meeting the requirements of both assessment criteria. The table below summarises how each appears in effective academic writing.

Analysis involves	Evaluation involves	Discussion involves
• breaking down information and examining its components to understand meaning • interpreting data, identifying patterns and explaining how elements relate to each other • asking 'What does this mean?' and 'How does it work?' Example: In a literature essay, analysis might examine how specific imagery contributes to a poem's theme.	• making reasoned judgments about quality, significance or validity using specific criteria • assessing strengths and limitations, acknowledging alternative viewpoints, and reaching conclusions about importance • asking 'What is the value or significance?' and 'How reliable or valid is this?' Example: In a science essay, evaluation might assess the reliability of experimental methods, the validity of results, and the significance of findings within the field.	• connecting analysed findings to broader contexts and perspectives • exploring relationships between ideas, comparing different viewpoints and considering implications • addressing 'How does this relate to other ideas?' and placing findings in conversation with existing scholarship Example: A history essay discussion might compare the student's interpretation of a primary source with how different historians have viewed.

These three elements build upon each other: analysis interprets meaning, discussion connects to broader contexts, and evaluation makes judgments about significance and validity.

Analysis versus description

Students must not stray into description or reporting as they write their body paragraphs. There are several reasons that this tends to happen. They may:

- be unsure of the difference between analysis and summary
- be in a hurry, so they summarise because it is faster and easier to do that than to deeply engage with and think through the material
- be uncomfortable with or unsure about the information
- assume the reader understands what the evidence means.

To ensure that they are analysing, ask them to imagine their reader asking, after every point they make, 'Why?' and 'So what?' or 'How does this relate to your overall point?' They can also check they have written analytically by looking at each point they have made and writing a sentence after it that begins, 'This matters because ...' or 'This shows ...' and then finishing those sentences. (They can remove those stems in their actual essay because what will follow should be able to stand on its own.)

Example

Jan is writing a Global Politics essay. Here is a paragraph he wrote about India's development:

'India has increased its naval presence in the Indian Ocean region. Many island nations, such as the Maldives and Sri Lanka, have signed maritime agreements. These deals include port access and joint patrols. Some countries are shifting their partnerships from China to India.'

This paragraph presents information but does not offer any analysis. Jan tries adding 'This shows...' or 'This matters because...' after each statement:

'India has increased its naval presence in the Indian Ocean region. This shows how emerging powers can project influence without aggressive military action.

Many island nations, such as the Maldives and Sri Lanka, have signed maritime agreements. This matters because these small island nations are strategically located along crucial maritime trade routes.

These deals include port access and joint patrols. This shows how India is creating a network of friendly ports to establish itself as the region's primary security partner.

Some countries are shifting their partnerships from China to India. This matters because it demonstrates how smaller nations are re-evaluating their diplomatic alignments based on geographic and cultural proximity.'

Jan then deletes or minimises the pure description with which he began, keeping the statements that follow 'because' and 'this shows' and then connecting them. He combines the above and ends up with this paragraph:

'India's expansion of naval presence demonstrates how emerging powers can project influence through diplomatic means rather than military pressure. The strategic targeting of island nations reveals India's broader aim to secure crucial maritime trade routes. By establishing a network of friendly ports, India transforms geographic proximity into diplomatic leverage. The shifting alignments of smaller nations from China to India illustrates the growing importance of cultural and historical ties in regional security partnerships.'

He then develops these analytical points further by asking 'So what?' Doing so forces him to think through his argument more deeply and yields a more sophisticated discussion. His final version read like this:

'India's naval cooperation across the Indian Ocean shows how emerging powers can establish regional dominance through "soft" maritime diplomacy instead of military force. Joint patrols and port agreements serve as strategic measures against external influence in what India considers its maritime territory. By becoming the primary security partner for smaller island nations, India converts its geographical position into diplomatic advantage, creating a buffer zone against competing powers. Providing naval assistance to states previously aligned with China demonstrates how India uses its democratic identity and trade history to present itself as a preferable regional partner. This strengthens India's position as the leader of Indian Ocean security, while highlighting the balance smaller states must maintain between regional powers.'

Evaluation and discussion

The example above demonstrates effective analysis – breaking down information and explaining its significance to support a claim. For discussion and evaluation (Criterion D), the student also needs to:

- discuss the broader significance of these findings
- consider alternative interpretations
- assess strengths and limitations of their research approach
- explain implications beyond their specific example.

Below are two examples of effective discussion and evaluation.

Example

Subject: IB Literature and IB Psychology (interdisciplinary pathway)

Research question: 'To what extent do domestic pressures contribute to female psychological deterioration in Euripides' *Medea* (431 BC) and Gillian Flynn's *Gone Girl* (2012), and how do these works, despite their historical separation, present parallel critiques of the psychological impact of gender expectations on women?'

Discussion and evaluation: While this investigation effectively establishes parallels between Medea's and Amy Dunne's psychological deterioration within their domestic spheres, certain limitations must be acknowledged. The analysis relies heavily on feminist literary theory, particularly Betty Friedan's concept of 'the problem that has no name' which, while helpful, may oversimplify the complex contexts of Ancient Greece and modern America. A broader theoretical framework incorporating historical perspectives on women's roles in Ancient Greek society could have provided deeper insights into Medea's actions.

Additionally, the investigation might have benefited from examining a wider range of contemporary psychological research on domestic pressure and mental health, which could have strengthened the connections drawn between societal expectations and psychological breakdown. The comparison between these texts, separated by more than two millennia, also raises questions about the universality of female experience that could have been more thoroughly addressed. Despite these limitations, the investigation's focus on close textual analysis of specific scenes where domestic pressures manifest in violent thoughts or actions has yielded valuable insights into how both authors portray the relationship between domesticity and psychological stability. In addition, the consideration of real-world psychological studies of the same issue has helped illuminate the psychological state of each heroine. Future study might explore the limitations of fiction on the understanding of psychological conditions.

Example

Subject: IB History

Research question: 'To what extent did the implementation of the Marshall Plan in Italy between 1948 and 1952 worsen regional economic disparities between the industrial north and rural south?'

Discussion and evaluation: This investigation of the Marshall Plan's implementation in Italy (1948–1952) demonstrates that economic aid alone did not drive Italy's post-war recovery. Rather, the evidence suggests that the Plan's success stemmed from its integration with domestic political reforms and social programmes, particularly in the industrial north. The analysis of previously overlooked regional economic data reveals significant disparities in aid distribution, with northern regions receiving 48% more per capita funding than the south, as noted above. While American diplomatic records portray the Plan as purely economic assistance, Italian government archives suggest it was deliberately used to strengthen anti-communist political forces, especially in industrial centres. These findings challenge traditional interpretations that emphasise the Plan's economic rather than political impact. This investigation thus contributes to our understanding of how international aid programmes can both solve and create domestic challenges, while highlighting the importance of examining economic policies through both political and social lenses.

Insight

'When I started my extended essay, I thought analysis was just explaining my data, discussion was talking about it more, and evaluation was saying if it was good or bad. But what I've learned is that analysis requires me to interpret what my findings actually mean, discussion involves putting my findings in conversation with existing research, and evaluation demands that I make reasoned judgments about the significance and limitations of my work based on clear criteria'.

Ruth-Anne B., IB Diploma Programme candidate

Structure and formatting

Below are the IB's requirements for the format of the essay.

General formatting

- 12-point font size
- 1.5 line spacing
- Page numbers beginning with the first page after the Table of contents page
- No identifying marks anywhere in the essay (student name, supervisor's name, school or institution's name, and so on)
- File size no larger than 10 MB (if there are high-resolution graphics in the essay or other embedded images, they may need to be condensed)

Title page

- IB student code
- Research question
- Title (optional)
- Subject-focused or interdisciplinary essay, stating the Diploma Programme subject of the essay (such as Psychology or Visual Arts) or the interdisciplinary subjects and the framework it connects to
- Word count (note: if the essay includes footnotes with anything other than citation information, include the following clarification: 'the stated word count includes explanatory footnotes')

Table of contents

This should reflect the subsections of the essay. If there are explicit subheadings in the essay, the student should use those. If there are not, it is helpful to create some to reflect the content of the essay – enough to give the reader a sense of the essay's organisation and a preview of its contents.

The essay

- Introduction (page numbering begins on the first page of the introduction)
- Body
- Conclusion

Works cited or References

The name of this page depends on the citation style chosen (IB does not specify a particular citation style, although your school may).

Appendices

If applicable (this section might include material such as a copy of a survey distributed to gather data in a science essay, or the complete text of poems discussed in a literature essay, if they are not commonly accessible).

Note that examiners are not required to read any appendices, so anything that is intended as part of the essay should be in the body of the essay itself.

Word count

Maximum of 4,000 words

Included in the word count	Not included in the word count
• Introduction • Main body • Conclusion • Quotations • Footnotes and/or endnotes that are not references	• Contents page • Headers • Maps, charts, diagrams, annotated illustrations • Tables • Equations, formulas and calculations • Citations/references (whether parenthetical, numbered, footnotes or endnotes) • Bibliography • Reflection and progress form

Academic writing guidance

In addition to enriching research skills, the extended essay also helps students develop their academic voices. As you have seen, the assessment criteria evaluate students on a variety of skills and competencies; by aligning supervision activities with specific criteria, you can provide targeted support that helps students excel in each area of assessment.

This guide offers academic writing support through three key tools: the 'Argument flow map' for structuring a focused line of reasoning, 'So what?' depth chains for developing analytical insight, and the 'Evaluation compass' for critically assessing sources and claims. These tools align with skills emphasised in the assessment criteria and can help students reflect on their proficiency as they begin writing.

Argument flow map

Ask students to use the following flow chart.

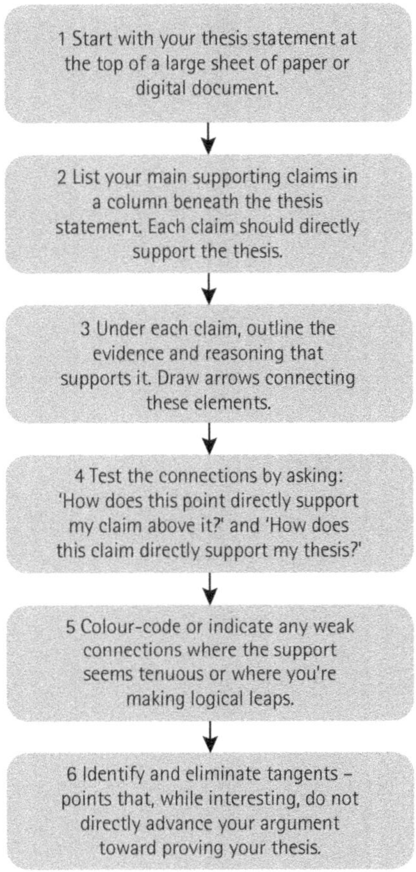

'So what?' depth chains

Direct students in the following way.

1 Start with an observation or result from research data or primary source.

2 Apply the 'So what?' question repeatedly to drill down through layers of significance:

- Level 1: What did I find? (Observation)
- Level 2: *So what* does this mean? (Interpretation)
- Level 3: *So what* does this matter in relation to my thesis? (Significance)
- Level 4: *So what* does this reveal about the broader field? (Implications)
- Level 5: *So what* might this suggest for future understanding? (Extension)

3 Document each level on separate sticky notes or in a chain diagram.

Evaluation compass

Direct students in the following way.

1 Create an 'evaluation compass' either on paper or digitally, with four key directions:
- North: Strengths – what is powerful about this finding/argument?
- South: Limitations – what weaknesses or gaps are there?
- East: Alternative perspectives – how might others view this differently?
- West: Implications – what are the consequences or applications?

2 For each major finding or argument, fill in all four compass points with specific, substantive responses.

3 Add compass 'inter-cardinal points' for deeper evaluation:
- Northeast: Potential for further development.
- Southeast: Methodological considerations.
- Southwest: Contextual factors affecting interpretation.
- Northwest: Connection to existing scholarship.

Apply the compass to three or four key findings/arguments from the research. Finally, identify patterns across your evaluations and draft paragraphs that incorporate balanced evaluation.

> **Remember**
>
> To support learning, extended essay coordinators can plan targeted lessons like the examples here. Likewise, supervisors can use the questions detailed for each criterion in Chapter 4 to help students self-assess. Providing students with both 'good' examples and requiring them to fix 'bad' examples is helpful as well.

Reviewing the rough draft

When you read a student's rough draft, look for the following features of sophisticated academic writing. If any are lacking, use the questions provided to guide the student as they plan their revisions:

Precise language

(Avoiding vague, ambiguous, or overused words or phrases.)
- 'What specific terms in your field might better capture what you mean by [vague term]?'
- 'How might you rephrase this section to make your position more precise?'
- 'What patterns do you notice in the language used by scholars in this field?'
- 'Where in your draft do you feel your language could be more specific or concrete?'

Smooth integration of sources, quotes and evidence

(Rather than just dropping in quotations or using awkward phrasing.)
- 'How does this quotation connect to the point you are making in this paragraph?'
- 'What made you choose to quote rather than paraphrase here?'

- 'Where do you see your own voice most clearly in this section? Where does it fade?'
- 'How would you explain this author's idea in your own words while maintaining its meaning?'

Meaningful, relevant information

(Rather than unrelated or excessive summary or tangents.)

- 'How would you justify the space you have given to [this subtopic] in relation to your main question?'

Effective introduction, conclusion and flow

- 'How does this section advance your overall argument?'
- 'What connections do you see between your third and fourth sections that might not be explicit on the page?'
- 'If a reader only remembered one thing from each section, what would you want that to be?'
- 'Where do you feel the logical flow of your argument might get interrupted?'
- 'What context does your reader need to understand why this research question matters?'
- 'What broader implications of your findings are not yet articulated in your conclusion?'
- 'How has your understanding of the question evolved since you began your research?'
- 'What surprised you in your research that might also surprise your reader?'

> **Remember**
>
> Supervisors are not permitted to edit student work or prescribe changes but, rather, to provide feedback and use open-ended questioning to allow the student to do the 'heavy-lifting' of revision.

Citing, referencing and ethical research

Remind students that academic integrity and ethical research practices are fundamental to good scholarship, and that their extended essay is their 'ambassador' – it should represent them well, not just by high-quality work but with honesty and integrity. They should understand how and when to cite sources or to otherwise give credit to others' work and assistance.

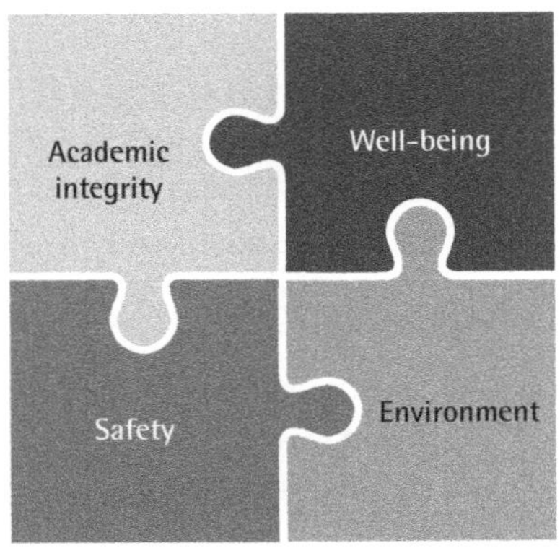

The IB invites students to think of ethical research as a four-piece puzzle. Each piece matters, and they all work together.

Academic integrity

Citation and referencing

The IB does not mandate a particular citation style for extended essays. It is your school's choice if you prefer to require a standard citation style or if you will allow students to use the citation style that fits best with the subject or with which they feel most comfortable.

Citing AI use

Students should understand when and how to acknowledge any use of generative AI in their research process. While AI tools are not academic sources and should not be cited as such for factual claims or scholarly analysis, students may use them in limited ways – for example, during the initial stages of developing a research question or methodology. In such cases, students should be transparent with their supervisor and reflect on their use of AI in their RRS.

Formal citation is generally not required when AI tools are used to support early thinking or planning; however, if AI-generated content is quoted, paraphrased or referenced directly in the essay, then citation is necessary. Any such use should be carefully considered and used sparingly.

Because citation conventions for generative AI are still evolving, you should encourage students to consult current guidance from official style guides such as MLA, APA and Chicago. Reliable resources such as the Purdue OWL website are frequently updated and can serve as helpful references. Librarians and extended essay coordinators can also support students to make informed decisions about acknowledging AI tools. Encouraging transparency and staying informed ensures students uphold the principles of academic integrity throughout the research process.

Well-being

Some research topics may be sensitive or challenging for students or others involved in the research. If a student is working with a potentially sensitive topic, help them to approach the subject responsibly and appropriately. Remind them that research should respect privacy, cultural contexts and individual perspectives – for example, medical confidentiality, socioeconomic sensitivity when conducting research among peers, or dealing with religious beliefs.

Safety

If a student's research involves other people, they must obtain their **informed consent** and protect their privacy. For research involving experiments or fieldwork, particularly in sciences, there are specific safety guidelines. Subject area teachers can provide these, and students must follow them carefully.

Environment

The IB is committed to thoughtful awareness of how work and research may affect the environment. Consider asking students these types of questions to encourage their awareness of their impact:

- Have you considered how your research methods might impact the environment? What steps can you take to minimise any negative effects?
- If you are conducting fieldwork, what precautions will you take to avoid disturbing natural habitats or ecosystems?
- How might you make more sustainable choices in your research process regarding materials and resources?
- Are there any specific environmental concerns unique to your research topic or methodology that should be addressed?
- How might you incorporate sustainable practices when collecting or analysing data?
- Have you researched any environmental guidelines or best practices that relate specifically to your field of study?

- In what ways could your research potentially contribute to environmental awareness or sustainability?
- What small changes could you implement in your research routine that would reduce your environmental footprint?

Good practices to share with students regarding ethical research

✓ Keep detailed records of your sources in your RRS.

✓ Cite as you write rather than trying to add citations later.

✓ Be clear about what help you have received from others.

✓ When in doubt about whether to cite something, cite it.

✓ Ask your supervisor if you are unsure about any ethical issues.

✓ Consider the impact of your research on others and the environment.

✓ Follow all safety guidelines carefully.

✓ Make sustainable choices where possible.

Commitment to success

The writing and revision part of the extended essay may pose challenges for students, so coordinators and supervisors are crucial during this phase. Thoughtful skill-targeting and review of student work in progress will make a huge difference. And remember: through your guidance on academic writing, you are teaching students to organise thoughts, evaluate evidence, and articulate complex ideas – skills that will serve them throughout their lives.

Key takeaways: Chapter 10

- You can help students develop sophisticated writing techniques such as following a focused line of argument, performing deep analysis, and evaluating sources through targeted activities and open-ended questioning.
- The essay should include a well-crafted introduction with research question and context, body paragraphs that build upon each other with analysis, and a conclusion that synthesises findings and connects to broader implications.
- Students must distinguish between analysis, evaluation, and discussion: analysis interprets meaning by examining components, evaluation makes judgments about quality and significance, and discussion connects findings to broader contexts and perspectives.
- Ethical research practices are fundamental: students should understand proper citation (including any AI use), consider the well-being of research participants, follow safety guidelines, and be environmentally conscious in their research methods.

Key terms

informed consent: ensuring that all participants in research understand the nature of the study, any potential risks, and their right to withdraw at any time

research methods: the specific techniques, tools and procedures used to collect and analyse data, such as surveys, experiments or textual analysis

Appendix

Guidance for conducting reflection meetings

Initial meeting

1. Begin by explaining your role as a supervisor to the student – you are there to guide and support, not to write the essay or make decisions for them. Clarify that while you will provide structure and feedback, they maintain ownership of their work. Establish your working relationship, set expectations, and so on.
2. Ask open-ended questions, such as the following, to get the student talking about their topic and to help you understand why they have chosen it and how they are feeling.
   - ❏ What has drawn you to this research topic, and what preliminary knowledge do you already have about it?
   - ❏ What do you know already about studies in this subject or subjects, and what do you need to learn more about (for example, methods and methodology)?
   - ❏ Have you formulated a working research question that aligns with your subject's or subjects' criteria and promotes analytical thinking?
   - ❏ How familiar are you with the extended essay requirements for your chosen subject area(s), and have you reviewed the relevant sections of the extended essay guidance?
   - ❏ Which pathway will you choose, and can you articulate why this pathway is the best choice for your topic?
   - ❏ What key sources have you identified so far, and what is your strategy for finding additional reliable resources?
   - ❏ What theoretical frameworks or methodologies are you planning to use, and are you aware of any ethical considerations related to your research?
   - ❏ Have you read and do you understand the assessment criteria?
   - ❏ What challenges have you encountered in your process thus far, and what steps are you taking to address them?
   - ❏ How are you organising your RRS, and what types of materials are you including to document your thinking process?
   - ❏ What timeline have you established for research, writing and revision, and how will you manage your time effectively?
   - ❏ What specific goals do you have between now and our next meeting?
   - ❏ How are you ensuring that your research approach is analytical rather than merely descriptive?
   - ❏ What steps are you taking to maintain balance during this process?

3. Confirm that students have read and understood relevant materials such as the extended essay guide, subject-specific criteria and requirements, rules regarding ethical research practices, and so on. Make sure they understand scholarly research and how to establish and maintain an organisation system. Help them set goals for the entire process.
4. End by assigning clear next steps based on your discussion, such as:
   - ❑ refining their research question
   - ❑ identifying initial or additional sources
   - ❑ creating a preliminary outline
   - ❑ setting the date for your next check-in (and reminding them to come prepared with questions and an agenda)
   - ❑ composing a reflection in their RRS (which can provide material later for the reflective statement).
5. Document this meeting on the RPF.

Interim meeting

1. Begin by chatting about how the process is going and how the student is feeling. At this stage, students should have made substantial progress but still have time to adjust course if needed.
   - ❑ Review their research question – has it evolved or been refined since the first meeting?
   - ❑ Examine how their methodology is working in practice.
   - ❑ Evaluate the quality and quantity of sources they have gathered.
   - ❑ Check their progress against the timeline established in the first meeting.
2. Below are some questions you might ask to encourage the student to discuss not only the work they are doing but also what they are learning (about both the topic and themselves). This is also a good time to remind them to think about the significance of their work and renew their motivation.
   - ❑ What progress have you made in your research so far, and how have you managed your approach?
   - ❑ What obstacles have you encountered, and how have you overcome them? (These might be academic challenges or they might relate to self-management skills.)
   - ❑ How are you maintaining your academic integrity and ensuring your work remains your own?
   - ❑ Has your research question evolved, and how has your understanding of the topic deepened or changed?
   - ❑ What adjustments to your research plan are necessary to successfully complete your essay?
   - ❑ How well are you satisfying the assessment criteria?
   - ❑ How coherent is your argument structure, and does it provide clear logical progression throughout?
   - ❑ Have you included sufficient evidence to support your claims, and have you critically evaluated this evidence?
   - ❑ What inconsistencies or weaknesses have you identified in your analysis that need addressing?
   - ❑ Are you spending more time analysing, discussing and evaluating than simply summarising, describing or reporting?
   - ❑ Will a reader be able to easily follow your reasoning from introduction to conclusion?
   - ❑ What are you learning about the subject(s), research, your topic, writing, and so on?
   - ❑ What connections can you make between your extended essay and your other coursework or the real world?

3. You may also:
   - ❑ address any challenges or roadblocks they are facing
   - ❑ help them develop contingency plans if parts of their research are not working out
   - ❑ redirect if they are going off track or their scope has become too broad/narrow.
4. End by assigning clear next steps based on your discussion, such as:
   - ❑ establishing clear expectations for final draft submission
   - ❑ setting concrete goals for the next phase of their work
   - ❑ confirming the timeline for the remainder of the process
   - ❑ composing a reflection in their RRS (which can provide material later for the reflective statement).
5. Document this meeting on the RPF.

Viva voce

1. Explain that this is both an assessment opportunity and a chance for reflection. Ensure that the student can discuss their final essay knowledgeably so that you can finalise your authentication of their work.
2. Remind students to take a moment and celebrate their success upon completion of the essay.
3. Remember this informs their reflective statement, which they will compose after this meeting. Ask the kinds of questions that will help them write an effective reflection:
   - ❑ To what extent has your thinking about your subject, topic and research question changed and why do you think this is so?
   - ❑ What do you feel most proud of and why?
   - ❑ If you were to repeat this process, what would you do differently, and why?
   - ❑ What have you learned about yourself as a result of this process?
   - ❑ What were some transformative moments for you (positive, negative or both)? What were the particular 'peaks' and 'valleys' that you might use as examples to illustrate your growth?
   - ❑ How has this process prepared you for future study or work?
   - ❑ What abilities, knowledge or skills might you take from this and how might you use them in the future?
4. End by congratulating them on completing this significant academic milestone.
5. Document this meeting on the RPF.

Helping students set and meet goals throughout the process

At the beginning of each phase of the process, have students identify *two achievable goals* for the phase. At the halfway and end point of each one, assign an RRS reflection in which students assess themselves honestly and identify steps for improvement, if needed.

Before you begin

1. Introduce the concept: Explain that research projects succeed through incremental progress rather than last-minute work. Goals create accountability and direction.
2. Define the phases: Break the extended essay process into clear phases:
   - Topic exploration and question formulation
   - Research gathering
   - Outline development
   - First draft writing
   - Revision and feedback incorporation
   - Final editing and submission
3. Timeline clarity: Provide clear dates for the beginning, midpoint and end of each phase.
4. Goal criteria: Goals should be SMART (specific, measurable, achievable, relevant, time-bound).

Facilitating effective goal-setting

Below are some examples of achievable goals by phase (your school may have different interim deadlines or phases).

Topic exploration phase:

- Read and annotate three scholarly articles related to the subject area.
- Complete two interviews with subject matter experts.
- Develop three potential research questions with justifications for each.

Research gathering phase:

- Collect and organise notes from eight academic sources.
- Create a system for tracking bibliographic information.
- Identify gaps in research and find two sources to address them.

Outline development phase:

- Complete a detailed outline with supporting evidence for each section.
- Create a visual map connecting the main arguments.
- Schedule and complete a consultation with librarian.

First draft phase:

- Write 500 words per day for eight days.
- Complete the introduction and two body sections.
- Create all necessary visuals/diagrams/tables.

Revision phase:

- Address all supervisor feedback points.
- Improve transitions between three key sections.
- Strengthen conclusion by connecting to broader implications.

Final editing phase:

- Review all citations for accuracy and consistency.
- Complete final formatting check against IB requirements.
- Have peer review for clarity and coherence.

Self-assessment process (APE reflection)

Guide students to use this assess, ponder, evolve (APE) framework at midpoint and endpoint reviews, and enter their reflections in their RRS:

Assess:

- What were my specific goals for this phase?
- What progress have I made towards each goal? (quantify when possible)
- Where do I stand in relation to the broader extended essay timeline?

Ponder:

- Why did I achieve/not achieve my goals?
- What unexpected challenges or opportunities arose?
- What am I learning about my research/writing process?
- How does this phase connect to my overall extended essay vision?

Evolve:

- What specific actions will I take to address any shortfalls?
- Do I need to adjust my approaching goals?
- What resources or support would help me move forward?
- What will I do differently in the next phase?

Cultivating a reflective mindset

The following activities will help students cultivate a reflective mindset throughout the extended essay process.

1 Start, stop, continue

This activity will encourage productive reflection at several points in the process: after initial research, following the first draft, during mid-process check-ins, after receiving supervisor feedback and before final submission.

Have students draw three columns or sections labelled 'Start', 'Stop' and 'Continue'. They should set aside 15–20 minutes of uninterrupted time. They should have their extended essay materials, feedback and notes accessible. For each category, have students ask themselves the following questions.

Start: What should I begin doing that I have not tried yet?

- ❑ New research methods or sources to explore
- ❑ Different writing approaches
- ❑ More efficient organisational systems
- ❑ Additional meetings with my supervisor
- ❑ New time-management techniques

Stop: What activities or approaches are not working and should be discontinued?

- ✕ Unproductive research 'rabbit holes'
- ✕ Ineffective note-taking methods
- ✕ Procrastination patterns
- ✕ Sources that are not yielding useful information
- ✕ Unfocused writing sessions

Continue: What is working well that I should maintain?

- ✓ Effective research strategies
- ✓ Productive writing routines
- ✓ Helpful resources
- ✓ Successful time-management techniques
- ✓ Valuable collaboration with my supervisor

Tip

Tell students to:

- be specific in their reflections (for example 'Start using Cornell notes method' rather than 'Start taking better notes')
- limit each category to 3–5 items to keep goal actionable
- create concrete next steps for each item
- share their reflections with their supervisor to get additional input
- schedule a follow-up review to assess progress on implementing changes.

This structured reflection process helps students systematically improve their approach while creating documentation of their evolving process, which is valuable evidence for the reflective statement.

2 Small group reflection sessions

Schedule times (once every month to six weeks, for example) for students to discuss progress, challenges and discoveries together. You may wish to group students by subject area or randomly. Give them structured but open-ended questions to ask each other. Some examples are given below.

Initial stages:

- What aspect of your research topic excites you the most right now?
- What was the most unexpected discovery you have made so far in your preliminary research?
- How has your research question evolved since you first started thinking about it?
- What resource has been most valuable to you at this stage?
- Are there any 'lessons learned' you think it would be helpful for others to hear, or advice for your group members?

Research process:

- What strategy has been most effective for you in organising your research?
- What is one research challenge you are currently facing that others might help with?
- How are you balancing primary and secondary sources in your research?
- What is one research method you have tried that others might benefit from hearing about?
- Are there any 'lessons learned' you think it would be helpful for others to hear, or advice for your group members?

Writing:

- Which section of your essay feels strongest to you right now, and why?
- What writing technique are you finding most challenging (thesis development, transitions, citations, etc.)?
- How are you approaching the structure of your argument?
- What feedback from your supervisor has been most helpful for your writing?

Personal process:

- What time-management strategy is working best for you right now?
- How do you get yourself back on track when you feel stuck or unmotivated?
- What has been your biggest 'Aha!' moment in this process so far?
- How has your understanding of academic research changed since beginning this project?
- Are there any 'lessons learned' you think it would be helpful for others to hear, or advice for your group members?

Critical thinking:

- What assumption did you have about your topic that has been challenged?
- How are you ensuring you are considering multiple perspectives in your research?
- What is one concept or methodology from your subject area that you are applying in a new way?
- How are you addressing limitations or weaknesses in your research?

End of the process:

- What aspect of this process has taught you the most about yourself as a student?
- How might what you are learning through this research connect to your future academic or career interests?
- What advice would you give to students just starting the extended essay process?
- What is a skill you have developed during this process that you think will be valuable beyond this assignment?

3 Non-traditional reflection activities and prompts

Students may come to see reflection as just another task they must complete, so break up regular reflections with more creative formats that can shake up their thinking. Here are some examples – you might choose to give students choice regarding format in order to increase agency and buy-in:

- Write a short 'sales pitch' explaining and inspiring interest in your topic to an imagined stranger.
- Represent your current mindset, your journey so far and your challenges and achievements. You may do so in the form of a song playlist; a series of photos or drawings; a weather report; a roadmap with landmarks, detours, and destinations; or a 'breaking news' series of headlines.
- Write a letter to your past or future self about the extended essay.
- Create a 'Then I thought ... Now I know ...' table documenting how your understanding about anything (subject-related or personal) has evolved.
- 'Critical friend' feedback exchange: Students pair up to ask challenging questions about each other's methodologies and conclusions.

Argument flow mapping

Creating an argument flow map can help students follow a focused line of argument in their extended essay. This visual technique allows them to trace their reasoning from beginning to end, and to identify any gaps or tangents.

Materials needed

- Large sheets of paper (A3 size works well) or digital tools like Miro, Jamboard or Lucidchart
- Coloured markers or pens
- Sticky notes (optional)
- Sample essays (optional)

Lesson plan

Step 1: Introduction

- ❑ Explain the concept of argument flow and why it matters for the extended essay.
- ❑ Show an example of a well-structured argument and a disconnected one.
- ❑ Show students a completed argument flow map using a sample essay or topic.

↓

Step 2: Guided practice

- ❑ Provide a sample thesis statement and supporting claims.
- ❑ Walk through creating a flow map together as a group.
- ❑ Discuss how to identify when points do not connect properly.

↓

Step 3: Individual mapping

- ❑ Have students write their thesis statement at the top of their paper/digital space.
- ❑ Ask them to list 3–5 main claims that support their thesis.
- ❑ For each claim, have them list specific evidence (quotes, data, examples).
- ❑ Draw arrows connecting evidence to claims, and claims to thesis.
- ❑ Add transition notes between sections.

↓

Step 4: Peer review

- ❑ Pair up students and ask them to exchange their maps.
- ❑ Provide a checklist for reviewers:
  - Does every element connect logically to what's above it?
  - Are there any claims without sufficient evidence?
  - Are there any interesting but tangential points?
  - Is the progression of ideas logical?

↓

Step 5: Reflection and revision

- ❑ Ask students to revise their maps based on the feedback.
- ❑ Get them to identify the strongest and weakest parts of their argument. They should colour-code sections as follows:
  - green (strong)
  - yellow (needs strengthening)
  - red (problematic/tangential)

↓

Step 6: From map to outline

- ❑ Guide students in converting their flow map into a formal essay outline.
- ❑ Show how each connection point can become a transition sentence.
- ❑ Demonstrate how to maintain the logical flow when expanding into paragraphs.

Tips

- Make this a recurring activity throughout the extended essay process.
- Have students revisit and revise their maps after drafting sections.
- Create a gallery walk where students can see others' mapping approaches.
- Provide examples of common flow problems and how to fix them.

Glossary

analysis: the process of breaking down information to examine relationships between elements, interpreting findings, identifying patterns, and explaining how evidence supports claims within a line of argument

artefact: a human-made object or creation that represents or reflects aspects of a culture, such as written documents, media productions (newspapers, magazines, films), artistic creations (works of fine art, architecture) and cultural expressions (fashion items, food dishes and brands) when analysed as manifestations of culture

authenticate: to verify that the work submitted by students is genuinely their own

best-fit approach: an assessment method where examiners determine which level descriptor most closely matches the quality of the student's work overall, recognising that not all aspects may perfectly fit a single level

Boolean operators: words or symbols such as 'and', 'not' and 'or', which are used to combine or exclude key words during an internet search to make the results more relevant and focused

collusion: a violation of academic integrity, when two or more students work together on an assignment that is to be submitted for individual assessment, trying to submit work that is not completely their own

criterion-referenced: An assessment approach that evaluates student work against established standards or criteria rather than comparing it to other students' performance

decision matrix: an analytical tool that evaluates options against multiple criteria to enable systematic decision-making

Digital Object Identifier (DOI): a unique alphanumeric code assigned to digital content that provides a permanent, reliable link to locate that content online (even if website content or address changes)

double-dipping: a violation of academic integrity, when a student attempts to submit material used for another IB assessment, such as part of the Biology IA for a Biology extended essay

evaluation: making judgments about the quality, value or significance of findings, considering strengths and limitations, weighing different perspectives and assessing the reliability and validity of evidence

frameworks: conceptual structures that organise thinking and provide contexts for understanding relationships between ideas

Gantt chart: a diagram or picture of the stages of a piece of work, showing stages that can be done at the same time and those that must be completed before others can begin

hallucination: AI-generated content that is factually incorrect, nonsensical, or not grounded in its training data or the information provided

holistically: considering all parts of something together rather than focusing on individual elements in isolation; in assessment, examining the complete work and how elements interact rather than evaluating separate components independently

IB continuum: the range of IB programmes for students from 3–19, which includes the Primary Years (PYP), Middle Years (MYP), Career Programme (CP) and the Diploma Programme (DP)

informed consent: ensuring that all participants in research understand the nature of the study, any potential risks, and their right to withdraw at any time

interdisciplinary: combining and integrating elements from two or more academic disciplines

Kanban board: a visual project management tool that helps students visualise work, track progress and optimise efficiency

metacognition: knowledge and understanding of your own thinking, processes and approaches to a skill or task

methodology: a broad theoretical framework and approach that justifies why certain research methods were selected and how they align with the research question

reflection and progress form (RPF): records of the mandatory reflection sessions, the student's reflective statement and the supervisor's authentication of the student's work; the RPF is submitted to IB along with the student's essay; a template is available in the Programme Resource Centre of the IB website

reflection session: a formal conversation between the student and their supervisor, which takes place three times throughout the process; these meetings are recorded in the RPF

reflective statement: a 500-word reflection written by the student after completion of the essay and viva voce, discussing and evaluating their experience during the extended essay process

research methods: the specific techniques, tools and procedures used to collect and analyse data, such as surveys, experiments or textual analysis

Researcher's Reflection Space (RRS): a dedicated place for the student to keep all their extended essay materials, from sources to research notes to reflections; the RRS can be digital or on paper, or a combination of the two

strand: a specific element or component within an assessment criterion that examiners evaluate; each criterion typically contains two or three strands that together determine the overall quality for that criterion

subject-specific pathway: an approach that explores a topic through the lens and methodologies of a single academic discipline

viva voce: (Latin 'with living voice') the final session or 'interview' between supervisor and student, in which the student makes an oral defence of the extended essay after the supervisor has read it; this also includes discussion and reflection on the process as a whole and what the student has learned, personally and about the topic